T0343041

Kid's Box

New Generation

Caroline Nixon &
Michael Tomlinson

CAMBRIDGE

Workbook
with Digital Pack

American English

5

Thanks and Acknowledgments

Authors' thanks

Many thanks to everyone at Cambridge University Press & Assessment for their dedication and hard work, and in particular to:

Louise Wood for doing such a great job overseeing the level; Catriona Brownlee for her dedication and sound editorial judgment; freelance editor Melissa Bryant.

We would also like to thank all our students and colleagues, past, present, and future, at Star English academy in Murcia, especially Jim Kelly for his friendship and support throughout the years.

Dedications

To Jim Kelly: Here's to the next thirty years of our Starship enterprise. – CN

To my Murcian family: Adolfo and Isabel, the Peinado sisters and their other halves for always treating me so well, thanks for being there and for making my life in Murcia so much fun. – MT

Illustrations

Ana Sebastian (Bright Agency); David Belmont, Javier Joaquin, Laszlo Veres, Moreno Chiacchiera (Beehive); Shahab (Sylvie Poggio Artists).

Audio

Audio production by John Marshall Media.

Design and typeset

Blooberry Design.

Additional authors

Rebecca Legros and Robin Thompson (CLIL); Montse Watkin (Sounds and life skills)

The authors and publishers acknowledge the following sources of copyright material and are grateful for the permissions granted. While every effort has been made, it has not always been possible to identify the sources of all the material used, or to trace all copyright holders. If any omissions are brought to our notice, we will be happy to include the appropriate acknowledgments on reprinting and in the next update to the digital edition, as applicable.

Key: U = Unit, V= Values

Photography

The following photos are sourced from Getty Images:

U0: Ableimages/DigitalVision; FatCamera/E+; Monty Rakusen/Image Source; Compassionate Eye Foundation/Martin Barraud/Stone; teekid/E+; mediaphotos/iStock/Getty Images Plus; Tom Werner/DigitalVision; John Harper/The Image Bank Unreleased; Hanna Hruts/iStock/Getty Images Plus; Tatyana Soloshenko/iStock/Getty Images Plus; photosynthesis/iStock/Getty Images Plus; Anna Erastova/iStock/Getty Images Plus; U1: metamorworks/iStock/Getty Images Plus; all images copyright of Jamie Lamb – elusive-images.co.uk/Moment; simonkr/E+; Chud/Moment; Dmytro Aksonov/E+; Zubkov/Moment; nndanko/iStock/Getty Images Plus; Thanapol Kuptanisakorn/EyeEm; Tracy Ducasse/Moment; Jacky Parker Photography/Moment; FARBAI/iStock/Getty Images Plus; Sudowoodo/iStock/Getty Images Plus; MicrovOne/iStock/Getty Images Plus; Aleksandra Alekseeva/iStock/Getty Images Plus; Vitalii Barida/iStock/Getty Images Plus; U2: Maskot; triloks/iStock/Getty Images Plus; Ben_Gingell/iStock/Getty Images Plus; SDI Productions/iStock/Getty Images Plus; Riska/E+; JGI/Jamie Grill/Tetra images; CasarsaGuru/E+; skynesher/E+; Thomas Northcut/DigitalVision; kali9/E+; Cavan Images; Westend61; adoc-photos/Corbis Historical; filmstudio/E+; Yellow Dog Productions/The Image Bank; David Madison/Stone; Marc Romanelli/Tetra images; Andrii Shablovskyi/iStock/Getty Images Plus; abadonian/iStock/Getty Images Plus; izusek/F+; Richard Drury/DigitalVision; miodrag Ignjatovic/E+; tomazl/E+; Yulia_Artemova/iStock/Getty Images Plus; Bubanga/iStock/Getty Images Plus; succodesign/iStock/Getty Images Plus; PeterSnow/iStock/Getty Images Plus; U3: Michael Blann/DigitalVision; Tomas Rodriguez/Stone; Nikada/E+; cglade/iStock/Getty Images Plus; By Eve Livesey/Moment; guvendemir/E+; Kypros/Moment; JGI/Tom Grill/Tetra images; ZoltanGabor/iStock/Getty Images Plus; Copyright Artem Vorobiev/ Moment Open; R.M. Nunes/iStock/Getty Images Plus; ollegN/iStock/Getty Images Plus; Sensvector/iStock/Getty Images Plus; veronawinner/iStock/Getty Images Plus; U4: George Diebold/Photodisc; Haje Jan Kamps/EyeEm; John Parrot/Stocktrek Images; Historical/Corbis Historical; Juanmonino/E+; Westend61; shannonstent/E+; Ascent/PKS Media Inc./Stone; Gary Yeowell/DigitalVision; traumlichtfabrik/Moment; George Pachantouris/Moment; paul gadd/The Image Bank; Carl & Ann Purcell/Corbis Documentary; Salvatore Virzi/EyeEm; Phathn Sakdi Skul Phanthu/EyeEm; artpartner-images/The Image Bank; reklamlar/iStock/Getty Images Plus; samxmeg/E+; Dorling Kindersley; Matt Mawson/Moment; Jeremy Woodhouse/Photodisc; U5: Pulse/Corbis; Petra Schueller/iStock/Getty Images Plus; OlegSam/iStock/Getty Images Plus; LinaTruman/iStock/Getty Images Plus; posteriori/E+; lilkar/iStock/Getty Images Plus; Metkalova/iStock/Getty Images Plus; cocodava/iStock/Getty Images Plus; frantic00/iStock/Getty Images Plus; Kyle Monk/Tetra images; piyaphat50/iStock/Getty Images Plus; chameleonseye/iStock/Getty Images Plus; Tatsuo115/iStock/Getty Images Plus; benedek/E+; Marina Inoue/Moment; Daniel_M/iStock/Getty Images Plus; Rajanish Kakade/AP; Blake Callahan/Moment; Jamroen Jaiman/EyeEm; Yoonjung Park/EyeEm; Deborah Cardinal/Moment Open; margouillatphotos/iStock/Getty Images Plus; StockFood/Foodcollection; Anna Blazhuk/Moment; Corbis/VCG; Dennis Welsh/UpperCut Images; Donald Iain Smith/Stone; John Howard/The Image Bank; View Pictures/Universal Images Group; ksana-gribakina/iStock/Getty Images Plus; U6: Caia Image/Collection Mix: Subjects; Klaus Vedfelt/DigitalVision; Marc Dufresne/iStock/Getty Images Plus; monstArrr_/iStock/Getty Images Plus; Zia Soleil/Stone; Robert Daly/OJO Images; Viktorcvetkovic/E+; GlobalP/iStock/Getty Images Plus; eli_asenova/E+; yusufsarlar/E+; vasileva/iStock/Getty Images Plus; bergamont/iStock/Getty Images Plus; luba/E+; Creative Crop/Photodisc; RedHelga/E+; Phill Thornton/iStock/Getty Images Plus; Pawel_B/iStock/Getty Images Plus; DustyPixel/E+; Wivoca/iStock/Getty Images Plus; choness/iStock/Getty Images Plus; TokenPhoto/E+; Thanee Chooha Noom/EyeEm; Easy_Asa/iStock/Getty Images Plus; IvanSpasic/iStock/Getty Images Plus; Mayur Kakade/Moment; Rob Van Petten/Photodisc; Francesco Riccardo Iacomino/Moment; Amarita/iStock/Getty Images Plus; KuznetsovDmitry/iStock/Getty Images Plus; Floortje/E+; courtneyk/iStock/Getty Images Plus; FG Trade/E+; Obaba/iStock/Getty Images Plus; Prostock-Studio/iStock/Getty Images Plus; Nikiteev_Konstantin/iStock/Getty Images Plus; Color_life/iStock/Getty Images Plus; peri priatna/iStock/Getty Images Plus; senkoumelnik/iStock/Getty Images Plus; owattaphotos/iStock/Getty Images Plus; U7: fizkes/iStock/Getty Images Plus; EcoPic/iStock/Getty Images Plus; Picture by Tambako the Jaguar/Moment; Steve Satushek/The Image Bank; Rawlinson_Photography/E+; miflippo/iStock/Getty Images Plus; Ian Peter Morton/iStock/Getty Images Plus; gremlin/E+; Byrdyak/iStock/Getty Images Plus; Denja1/iStock/Getty Images Plus; Christian Sanchez/500px Prime; mauricallari/iStock/Getty Images Plus; Jose Luis Pelaez Inc/DigitalVision; WOLFGANG KUMM/DPA; doomko/iStock/Getty Images Plus; prahprah/iStock/Getty Images Plus; Yulia Zelinskaya/iStock/Getty Images Plus; Jasius/Moment; U8: LanaStock/iStock/Getty Images Plus; Vesnaandjic/E+; DeanDrobot/iStock/Getty Images Plus; PeopleImages/iStock/Getty Images Plus; shishir_bansal/iStock/Getty Images Plus; Ascent Xmedia/Stone; Zero Creatives/Image Source; Maxian/E+; Barry Austin/DigitalVision; Nancy Honey/Photodisc; Peathegee Inc/Tetra images; Image Source/Stockbyte; Prostock-Studio/iStock/Getty Images Plus; mbbirdy/E+; pyotr021/iStock/Getty Images Plus; Imgorthand/E+; Cavan Images; Janie Airey/Image Source; SDI Productions/E+; Spiritartist/E+; JulyVelchev/iStock/Getty Images Plus; artisteer/iStock/Getty Images Plus; motimeiri/iStock/Getty Images Plus; Arra Vais/iStock/Getty Images Plus; VladislavStarozhilov/iStock/Getty Images Plus; eli_asenova/E+; shapecharge/E+; Maskot/DigitalVision; fstop123/E+; tatyana_tomsickova/iStock/Getty Images Plus; Westend61; Pacharada17/iStock/Getty Images Plus; Natariis/iStock/Getty Images Plus; V12: Marisvector/iStock/Getty Images Plus; V34: Halfdark/fStop; V56: mikkelwilliam/iStock/Getty Images Plus.

The following photos are sourced from other libraries:

U1: Pictorial Press Ltd/Alamy Stock Photo; U7: Matthijs Kuijpers/Alamy Stock Photo.

Cover Photography by Tiffany Mumford for Creative Listening.

Commissioned photography by Stephen Noble and Duncan Yeldham for Creative Listening.

Contents

⭐ **Welcome to our blog** 4

Sounds and life skills 8

1 Time for TV 10

Sounds and life skills 14
Media: How can we make nature documentaries? 16
A2 Flyers Listening Part 5 17
18

2 People at work

Sounds and life skills 22
Social studies: How can we stay safe? 24
A2 Flyers Reading and Writing Part 6 25
Review: units 1 and 2 26

3 City life 28

Sounds and life skills 32
Geography: What are the best modes of transportation? 34
A2 Flyers Listening Part 2 35

4 Disaster! 36

Sounds and life skills 40
Geography and history: Where can we find volcanoes? 42
A2 Flyers Reading and Writing Part 2 43
Review: units 3 and 4 44

5 Material things 46

Sounds and life skills 50
Art: What can you make with recycled materials? 52
A2 Flyers Listening Part 3 53

6 Senses 54

Sounds and life skills 58
Science: How do we make noises? 60
A2 Flyers Reading and Writing Part 5 61
Review: units 5 and 6 62

7 Natural world 64

Sounds and life skills 68
Geography: How can we help endangered species? 70
A2 Flyers Listening Part 1 71

8 World of sports 72

Sounds and life skills 76
Physical education: How do people train for different sports? 78
A2 Flyers Reading and Writing Part 4 79
Review: units 7 and 8 80

Values

Units 1 & 2: Respect in the classroom 82
Units 3 & 4: People who help us 83
Units 5 & 6: Tell the truth, but don't hurt 84
Units 7 & 8: Value your friendships 85
Grammar reference 86
Irregular verbs 88

Welcome to our blog

 1 Put the words in groups.

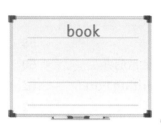

book

scarf

program

~~book~~   comic book
costume   internet
magazine   newspaper
~~program~~   ~~scarf~~
screen   sweater
sneakers   Wi-Fi

2 Match the sentences to Sally, Robert, and Eva.

1 (I had a good vacation.)   **2** (I'd like to write about sports.)   **3** (I didn't see you online.)

4 (I'm ready for a new school year.)   **5** (I'm sending you the information now.)   **6** (There's a competition for the best blog in the school.)

 ☐ ☐   ☐ ☐   1 ☐

 3 Read and complete.

blog   ~~diary~~   internet   music
online   pictures   sports   videos

A blog is a kind of (1) _____ diary _____ that you write
(2) _____. You can do a search and find one
on the (3) _____. You can read about soccer,
tennis, and other (4) _____. You can get
information about technology and the world around
us. You can look at a lot of really interesting
(5) _____, listen to all your favorite
(6) _____, and watch different kinds of
(7) _____. Robert, Sally, and Eva write the
new *Kid's Box* (8) _____. They want to win
the school blog competition. There's a great prize!

4 Correct the sentences.

1 A blog is a kind of book.
   No, it isn't. It's a kind of
   diary._____

2 You can find blogs in stores.
   _____
   _____

3 *Kid's Go* is a new blog.
   _____
   _____

4 The three writers are named
   Fahad, Lola, and Li Jing.
   _____
   _____

5 There's a prize for the worst blog.
   _____
   _____

Language: present simple questions and short answers   ▶ Do the online activities on **Practice Extra** as you complete this unit.

1 Read and order the text.

	blog for young people. There are
	are Eva, Robert, and
9	Eva likes the natural world and drawing. She
	don't have to go to school.
	things. Robert likes computers and sports, Sally
5	Sally. They all go to the same
	three writers. Their names
1	*Kid's Box* is an exciting new
	school: City School. They all like different
	really loves taking pictures, too. They write
	likes singing and music, and
	their blog on the weekend when they

2 Read and complete the questions.

| How many   What   ~~What's~~ |
| When   Where   Why |

1 _____What's_____ the blog called?

It's called *Kid's Box*.

2 _____ writers
are there?

There are three.

3 _____'s the blog about?

It's about the things that they like.

4 _____ do they write the blog?

They write it on the weekend.

5 _____ do they write it then?

They write it then because they
don't have to go to school.

6 _____ can you see the blog?

You can see it on the internet.

3 Write the correct sentences.

~~Sally would like~~	oldest of	the country.
Sally	to school	~~singing and music.~~
Eva walks	are both	Robert.
Robert's the	lives near	the children.
Eva	~~to write about~~	ten.
Sally and Eva	lives in	every day.

1 Sally would like to write about singing and
music.

2 _____

3 _____

4 _____

5 _____

6 _____

Choose the words from the box to label the pictures.

dictionary   test   geography   history   French   math   music   ~~science~~

1. science
2.
3.
4.
5.
6.

 Follow the school words.

classroom	ocean	back	beans	cave	eagle	rice
geography	history	potatoes	mountain	music	teacher	board
beard	math	English	knee	P.E.	lake	subject
salad	river	computer studies	turtle	art	soup	ears
mustache	yogurt	test	dictionary	science	elbow	field

Now complete the table with the words from Activity 2.

The body	Food	The natural world
elbow		

Two words are not like the others. What are they? _____

Which group are they from? _____

 Answer the questions.

1 What's your school called?   My school's called _____
2 What's your favorite subject?   _____
3 What was your first class yesterday?   _____
4 Do you have lunch at school or at home?   _____
5 What did you do after lunch yesterday?   _____
6 Did you have any homework yesterday?   _____

Read and complete the school schedule.

- Quinn has these classes at school: geography, history, music, math, English, P.E., computer studies, art, science.
- English is his last class on Mondays.
- His favorite day is Wednesday. He has P.E. at ten o'clock and music at eleven o'clock. He also has geography in the morning.
- On Thursdays, his history class finishes at four o'clock, and he has English at eleven o'clock.
- On Mondays, he studies a lot. Before lunch, he has math after science, and at eleven o'clock, he has computer studies. After lunch, he first has geography, and then he has history.

- Math is his last class on Tuesdays and Wednesdays.
- After science on Friday, Quinn has these classes in alphabetical order: history, P.E., computer studies, music, English.
- The first class on Mondays and Fridays is the second class on Tuesdays.
- On Tuesdays, the first class is computer studies. Before lunch, he has geography, and at two o'clock, he has P.E.
- He always has art after lunch, but not on Mondays or Fridays.
- He has music after art on Thursdays.
- He has science four times a week.

	Monday	Tuesday	Wednesday	Thursday	Friday
9:00–10:00				math	science
10:00–11:00					
11:00–12:00					
lunch					
13:00–14:00					
14:00–15:00			English		
15:00–16:00					

 Now write about Quinn's schedule on Monday.

On Monday,

 Write about your schedule on your favorite school day.

My favorite school day is

Sounds and life skills
Chatting with friends

Pronunciation focus

1 **Listen and circle the connected words.**

1 Hi. (How are) you?

2 How was your summer?

3 Are you happy to be back?

4 How about you?

5 Did you have fun?

2 **Listen and complete.**

Hi. (1) ___How___ ___are___ things?

Good thanks. (2) _____ you?

I'm fine, thanks. (3) _____ have a good summer?

It was great! We went to the beach for a vacation. How about you? (4) _____ do anything fun?

I went to soccer camp. It was amazing! (5) _____ happy to be back?

Yes, it's nice to see everyone.

3 **Read and match.**

1 What did you do for your vacation?
2 Did you go swimming?
3 Who did you go with?
4 How long did you stay there?
5 Was the weather nice?

a My family.
b We were there for a week.
c Yes, it was sunny every day.
d I went to the beach.
e Yes, I did. The ocean was great.

4 **Look at the picture of your friend. Write questions to ask him about his vacation.**

_____

_____

_____

1 Read and answer.

1 Who's older: Sir Doug or Diggory Bones? Sir Doug is older than Diggory.
2 How long is the model dinosaur? _____
3 What are Diggory's students learning about? _____
4 What did the Rosetta Stone help us do? _____
5 Where was Diggory's computer? _____

2 Read the text. Then look at the code and write the secret message.

Egyptian hieroglyphics were one of the first kinds of writing, but modern people couldn't understand them. Ancient people wrote important things on the Rosetta Stone in three different languages.

In 1822, a very smart man named Jean-François Champollion used two of the languages to understand the third, the Egyptian hieroglyphics. The Rosetta Stone helped us understand the past better.

a	b	c	d	e	f	g	h	i	j	k	l	m
n	o	p	q	r	s	t	u	v	w	x	y	z

V e r y _____ .

_____ .

Do you remember?

1 An internet diary is called a _____ blog _____ .
2 The children want to write a blog for their school _____ .
3 We use a _____ to find the meaning of words.
4 _____ is the school subject about different places in the world.
5 At school, we learn about plants and the human body in _____ .

Can do

I can talk about school subjects.

I can ask my friends about their school schedule.

I can write about my favorite school day.

1 Time for TV

What's the time?

It's six o'clock.

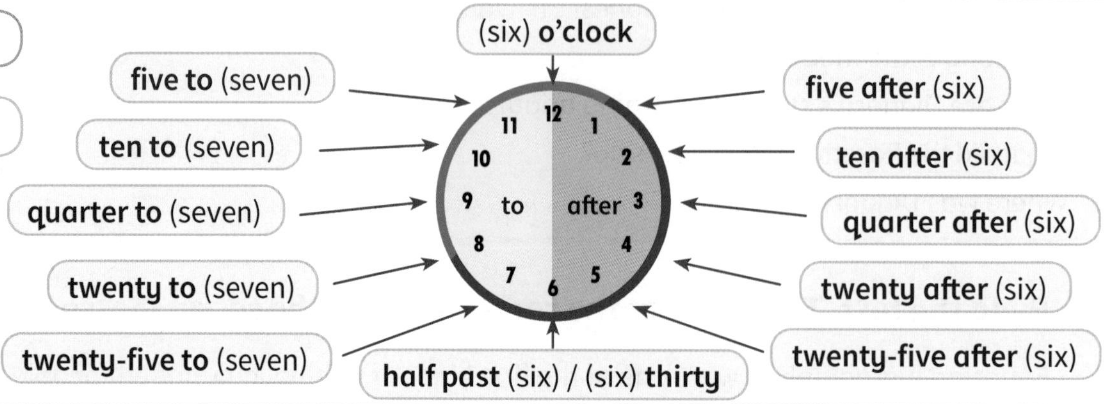

(six) o'clock

five to (seven)

ten to (seven)

quarter to (seven)

twenty to (seven)

twenty-five to (seven)

five after (six)

ten after (six)

quarter after (six)

twenty after (six)

twenty-five after (six)

half past (six) / (six) thirty

to   after

1 Match the clocks to the times.

1 ten to four

2 ten after four

3 five to four

4 quarter after four

5 twenty-five after seven

6 twenty after four

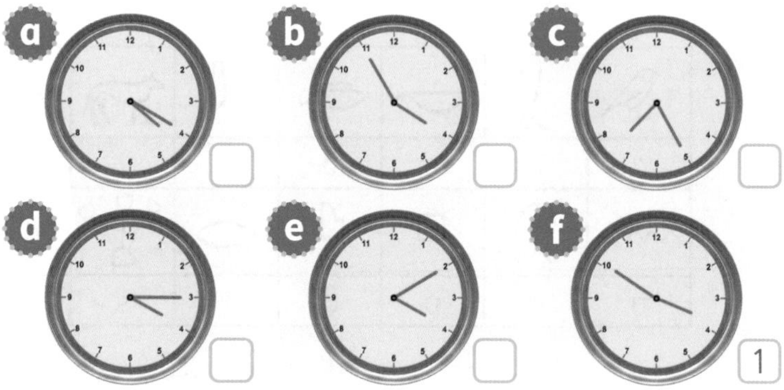

2 Look and write the times.

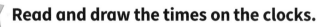

five after

eleven

3 Read and draw the times on the clocks.

1 David wakes up at 7:10 on Mondays, Wednesdays, and Fridays.

2 Nick leaves home at 8:55 in the morning.

3 Alex sometimes plays soccer at 15:30.

4 Anna always starts her homework at 16:00.

5 Akash watches his favorite show on TV at 18:45 on Tuesdays and Thursdays.

6 Petra goes to bed at 21:00 every night.

Do the online activities on Practice Extra as you complete this unit.

Match the clocks to the sentences for William's day yesterday. Put the sentences in order.

a He had lunch at half past twelve. ____

b Classes started again at quarter to two. ____

c He caught a bus to school at twenty-five after eight. ____

d School finished at four o'clock. ____

e William caught the bus home at ten after four. ____

f William got dressed at ten to eight. __1__

g He went out to the playground for recess at quarter to eleven. ____

h Classes began at nine o'clock. ____

 Find the past tense of these verbs and write them.

w	a	g	o	t	u	p	u
o	e	y	p	l	k	e	d
k	o	n	u	s	c	j	r
e	i	q	t	o	o	k	a
u	o	p	a	s	y	l	n
p	c	a	u	g	h	t	k
k	b	d	t	i	c	a	f
h	c	a	m	e	h	o	d

go _____went_____

come _____

have _____

catch _____

wake up _____

get up _____

eat _____

drink _____

put _____

take _____

 Answer the questions about yesterday.

1 What time did you get up?
   I got up at _____

2 What time did you go to school?
   _____

3 Where did you have lunch?
   _____

4 What time did you go home?
   _____

5 What did you eat for dinner?
   _____

6 What did you drink in the evening?
   _____

 Now write 20–30 words about what you did yesterday.

Yesterday, I _____

_____

Choose the words from the box to label the pictures.

cartoon   comedy   documentary   news   quiz show   series   sports   ~~weather~~

weather _____   _____   _____   _____   _____

 Write the shows.

1 On this show, you can see swimming, basketball, tennis, or motorcycle racing. _____sports_____

2 This show's funny, with funny people. _____

3 We watch this show to see if it's hot or cold today. _____

4 This is on every day. It's about important things around the world. _____

5 A show that tells us interesting facts about animals, history, or places. _____

6 This show has episodes and can be on TV every day. _____

 Read and answer the questions.

Channel 1	Channel 2	Channel 3	Channel 4
12:10 Fun House (cartoon) 1:00 The news 1:45 The weather 2:15 Chelsea vs. Milan (soccer) 4:15 Animals of Africa (documentary)	11:50 Top Songs (music videos) 12:30 Friendly (comedy) 2:10 Count to Ten (quiz show) 3:15 Giants vs. Bouncers (basketball)	12:30 The news 1:05 Explorers (documentary) 1:45 The weather 2:20 Annie (musical comedy movie) 3:45 Cartoon hour	1:15 Maskman Returns (movie) 2:30 Our Body (documentary) 3:15 Answer First (quiz show) 3:55 Laugh out Loud (comedy)

1 What time is the news on Channel 3? At 12:30. _____

2 What channels are the cartoons on? _____

3 What's on Channel 1 at quarter to two? _____

4 What are the names of the two quiz shows? _____ _____

5 What are the documentaries about? (1) _____ , (2) _____ , (3) _____

6 What time is the movie on Channel 4? _____

1 Read and complete the table.

It's now four o'clock. Four friends have a problem because they can't decide which show to watch.

- Sophia's favorite show starts in 20 minutes and is called *Quacky Duck*. She likes cartoons, but doesn't like documentaries or sports shows.
- The other girl, Petra, loves quiz shows.
- *Who Wants to Be a Billionaire?* started at 3:50.
- Frank loves playing sports, and he likes watching them, too. His favorite show starts in 45 minutes.

- The other boy's favorite show is called *World Around Us*. He's the only child who likes documentaries.
- The documentary starts at ten after four, and the cartoon starts at twenty after four.
- Deniz doesn't want to watch *Sunday Sports*.
- Finally they all decide to watch Petra's favorite show, but it started ten minutes ago!

Name	Sophia			
Kind of show				
Show name	Quacky Duck			
Show time				

2 Now answer the questions.

1 Who doesn't like documentaries? Sophia, Petra, and Frank
2 What's the name of the show they decide to watch? _____
3 When did it start? _____
4 Whose favorite show is it? _____
5 Who doesn't want to watch what's on TV at 4:45? _____
6 When does the cartoon start? _____

3 Answer the questions.

1 What's your favorite TV show?
My favorite TV show is _____

2 What kind of show is it?
_____

3 What time is it on?
_____

4 How many words can you find in "documentaries"?

star, mice, _____
_____
_____
_____
_____
_____

Sounds and life skills
Deciding together
Pronunciation focus

1 🎧 4 **Listen and write "1" and "2."**

a [2] sheep   [1] cheap
b [ ] share   [ ] chair   d [ ] ships   [ ] chips
c [ ] shoes   [ ] choose   e [ ] washes   [ ] watches

2 🎧 5 **Choose the words from Activity 1. Listen and check.**

1 The farmer bought _____cheap_____ _____sheep_____ .

2 The students had to _____ a _____ .

3 I have to _____ some new red _____ .

4 The sailors always eat potato _____ on the _____ .

5 Charlie _____ the children as she _____ her hands with soap.

3 🎧 6 **Read and write. Listen and check.**

> Can't you watch the race on your phone?   OK. I'll watch *Sing Up!* online later.
> ~~Ooh. *Sing Up!* is on in ten minutes.~~   Perfect!

Shannon: Ooh. Sing Up! is on in ten minutes.

Chuck: Oh! But I wanted to watch the Formula 1 race!

Shannon: _____

Chuck: Let me check. Yes, I can!

Shannon: _____

Chuck: Yes, but it's more exciting to watch on the big TV screen!

Shannon: _____

4 **Read and complete the TV questionnaire.**

1 _____How_____ _____many_____ **hours** of TV do you watch every week?
I watch ten hours every week.

2 _____ do you usually watch TV?
I usually watch TV around eight o'clock.

3 _____ do you watch TV?
I watch TV on the couch in my living room.

4 _____ _____ ever watch TV before school?
No, I don't. I don't have time!

1 Read and answer.

Diggory Bones

1 What's the Baloney Stone? It's a computer program of old languages.
2 Where's the Baloney Stone? _____
3 What time did Emily turn on the TV? _____
4 Which show did Diggory want to watch? _____
5 Who was the cameraman at the university? _____
6 What does Brutus Grabbe want? _____

2 Read the story so far and then write it in the past.

The story so far ...
Diggory's in a classroom at the university. The reporter and the cameraman arrive. The reporter asks Diggory some questions. Diggory says that he doesn't want the thief to use the Baloney Stone to find treasure. At half past nine, Diggory asks Emily to turn on the TV because he wants to watch the news. Brutus Grabbe comes onto the TV screen and laughs. He's the TV cameraman from the university! He wants Diggory's secret password for the computer program.

The story so far ...
Diggory was in a classroom at the university.
_____
_____
_____
_____
_____
_____

Do you remember?

1 The time in words is quarter to eleven. The time in numbers is ___10:45___.
2 The time in numbers is 8:25. The time in words is _____.
3 A _____ is a TV show that tells us interesting things about our world.
4 Two TV shows that usually make us laugh are _____ and _____.
5 Two words with "sh" (as in "show") are _____ and _____.
6 Two words with "ch" (as in "channel") are _____ and _____.

Can do

I can tell the time in English.

I can talk about different kinds of TV shows.

I can write about my favorite TV show.

How can we make nature documentaries?

1 Read and circle the adjectives.

Last week, I watched a (great) documentary called **Nature at Home**. It's about all the animals and insects that live in people's backyards. You can watch it on **DiscoveryPix**. I found it really interesting because there were a lot of insects in one place at one time. I loved watching the butterflies. They're so beautiful and colorful. The photography in the documentary is amazing. I know you enjoy nature shows, so you have to watch it.

2 Plan to write a chat message. Complete the information about a documentary.

13:02   56% 🔋

What did you watch?   Yesterday I watched _____.

What's it about?   It's about _____.

Where can you watch it?   You can watch it on _____.

What was it about?   Last night's episode was about _____.

What did you like about it?   I found it _____ because _____.

Why do people enjoy watching it?   People enjoy watching it because _____.

3 Use your notes to write a message to a partner about the documentary.

4 Did you ...

- ☐ plan your message?
- ☐ use adjectives to make it more interesting?
- ☐ read your message again?
- ☐ check grammar, spelling, and punctuation?

Writing tip

We use adjectives to describe things. You can use adjectives in your writing to make it more interesting.

You have to watch it because you can learn about **interesting** animals. The photography is **beautiful**, too!

Flyers Listening

Listen and color and write. There is one example.

2 People at work

We use *going to* to talk and write about the future.

Affirmative	Negative (n't = not)	Question
I'm **going to be** a nurse.	He **isn't going to be** a dentist.	**Is** he **going to be** an actor?
She's **going to visit** me.	We **aren't going to do** it.	**Are** they **going to clean** it?

1   Read and complete the sentences. ⎡ be   listen   play   read   ~~watch~~   wear ⎤

1   She's going to ____watch____ TV after school.

2   He's going to _____ a firefighter when he's older.

3   They aren't going to _____ a comic book.

4   We're going to _____ to pop music.

5   I'm going to _____ my new sneakers.

6   You aren't going to _____ badminton today.

2   Match the questions to the answers.

1   How are you going to find the street?   [e]
2   What time is he going to get up?   [ ]
3   Where are we going to have lunch?   [ ]
4   Who are they going to talk to?   [ ]
5   Which T-shirt are you going to wear?   [ ]
6   Why is he going to go to the music festival?   [ ]
7   When is she going to play basketball?   [ ]
8   What are they going to do after school?   [ ]

a   They're going to talk to their friends.
b   I'm going to wear my blue one.
c   We're going to have it at home.
d   He's going to listen to rock music.
e   We're going to look at a map.
f   He's going to get up at half past seven.
g   They're going to do their homework.
h   She's going to play on Saturday.

3   Look at this code. Write the secret message.

	1	2	3	4	5
1	a	b	c	d	e
2	f	g	h	i	j
3	k	l	m	n	o
4	p	q	r	s	t
5	u	v	w	x	y

a = 11, b = 21, c = 31

11–34–51   55–53–15   22–53–42–43–22   54–53   31–53–33–51
A r e   _____   _____   ____   _____

54–53   33–55   14–11–34–54–55?
____   ____   _____ ?

4 **Now write another message for a partner in your notebook.**

1 Look at the pictures and answer the questions.

1 What are they going to do?   They're going to wash their clothes.
2 What's she going to do?
3 What's he going to do?
4 What are they going to do?
5 What's he going to do?
6 What's she going to do?

2 Look and make negative sentences.

1 He isn't going to catch the bus.   4
2   5
3   6

3 Look at Tanaz's diary for the weekend. Ask and answer the questions.

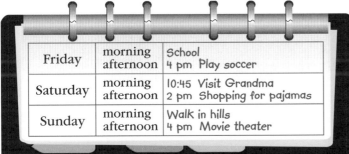

Friday	morning	School
	afternoon	4 pm Play soccer
Saturday	morning	10:45 Visit Grandma
	afternoon	2 pm Shopping for pajamas
Sunday	morning	Walk in hills
	afternoon	4 pm Movie theater

1 a Where / Tanaz / go / Friday morning
     Where is Tanaz going to go on
     Friday morning?
  b She's going to go to school.

2 a What / Tanaz / do / Friday afternoon

  b

3 a What time / Tanaz / visit her grandma

  b

4 a What / Tanaz / buy / Saturday afternoon

  b

5 a Where / Tanaz / walk / Sunday morning

  b

6 a What / Tanaz / do / Sunday afternoon

  b

Language: plans, intentions, and predictions with *going to*   19

Choose the words from the box to label the pictures.

actor   cook   dancer   designer
journalist   mechanic   ~~pilot~~   soccer player

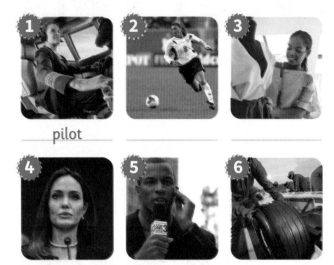

1 pilot

 Complete the table.

person	verb
teacher	teach
	drive
dancer	
	skate
	design
run	
	photograph
manager	
tennis player	
	swim

 Read and guess the jobs. Then write the words in the puzzle.

1 Someone who drives buses.
   A bus driver

2 Someone who works with food.
   A _____

3 Someone who stops fires.
   A _____

4 Someone who takes care of our teeth.
   A _____

5 Someone who works in a hospital.
   A _____

6 Someone who flies planes.
   A _____

7 Someone who repairs cars.
   A _____

8 Someone who paints pictures.
   An _____

9 Someone who acts in movies.
   An _____

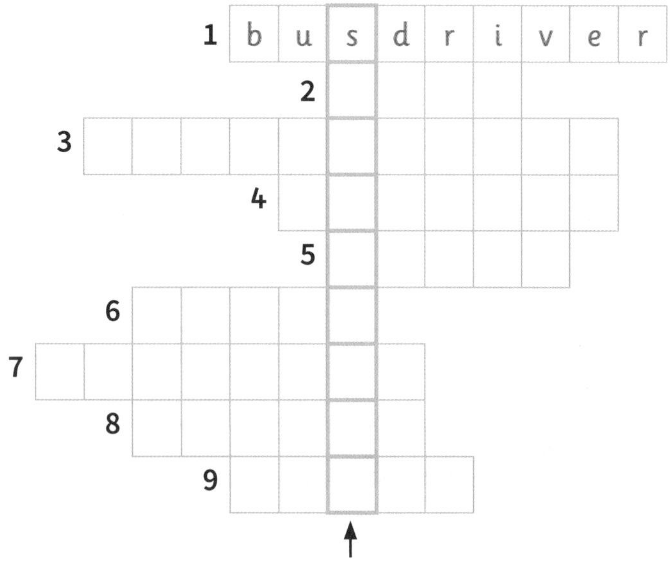

| 1 | b | u | s | d | r | i | v | e | r |

2
3
4
5
6
7
8
9

What's the mystery job? _____

 Now write a definition for this job.

_____

_____

These four children are going to have different jobs. Write the numbers.

 a

 b

 c

 d

a ☐ ☐ ☐   b ☐ ☐ ☐   c 1 ☐ ☐   d ☐ ☐ ☐

1 He's going to fly planes.
2 He's going to travel a lot.
3 He's going to repair cars.
4 She's going to use eggs.
5 He's going to get dirty.
6 She's going to wear a white hat.

7 He's going to visit a lot of airports.
8 She's going to work in a kitchen.
9 She's going to take care of people's teeth.
10 He's going to work with machines.
11 She's going to tell children not to eat candy.
12 She's going to wear gloves and a mask.

 Slim Jim's a famous singer. Read and complete his diary.

- He's going to meet his manager after lunch on Friday.
- On the same day that he sings, he's going to open a new school in the morning.
- He's going to go to the movies next Thursday afternoon.
- After lunch on the day he arrives in London, he's going to talk to some children who are in the hospital.
- He's going to do a TV interview before lunch on the day he goes to the movies.

- He arrives at London airport next Monday morning.
- On the same day that he's having dinner with some actors, he's going to visit a music store in the morning.
- He's going to sing in a big soccer stadium.
- He's flying to Spain on the morning of the same day that he's going to meet his manager.
- He's going to have dinner with some actors next Tuesday evening.

	Monday	Tuesday	Wednesday	Thursday	Friday
a.m.					
	lunch	lunch	lunch	lunch	lunch
p.m.					meet manager

 Answer the questions.

1 Where are you going to go after school this afternoon? I'm going to go _____

2 Who are you going to see this evening? _____

3 When are you going to do your homework? _____

4 What time are you going to go to bed tonight? _____

Vocabulary: jobs   21

Sounds and life skills
Thinking about the future

Pronunciation focus

 1 🎧 **8** **Listen and circle the /ər/ sounds. Then practice saying the sentences.**

1 I'm going to be a teach(er).
2 She wants to be a driver.

3 Maybe I can be a pop singer.
4 What are you going to be?

 2 🎧 **9** **Listen and complete.**

Emma

I think I'm going to be a ___writer___
when I'm _____.
I love cooking for _____.
Maybe I can be a food _____.

Oliver

I think I'm going to be a _____.
I can be your food _____.
Maybe sometimes I can be a
_____ in your restaurant.

 3 **Read and match.**

1 Loves children. Has to be creative and good at speaking English.
2 Loves animals. Has to be good at driving a tractor.
3 Is a good communicator. Has to love people and food.
4 Isn't scared in front of a lot of people. Has to be good at remembering words.
5 Is brave. Has to be good at climbing.

a an actor
b a farmer
c a firefighter
d a waiter
e an English teacher

 4 **How are these jobs similar and different? Read and complete.**

> cars   creative   take care of
> ~~outside~~   restaurant   stage

> actor   cook   dentist
> driver   ~~farmer~~   writer

1 farmer, firefighter, police officer
They all work ___outside___, but only
a ___farmer___ drives a tractor.

2 driver, engineer, mechanic
They all love _____, but only a
_____ drives one.

3 cook, manager, waiter
They all work with food in a _____,
but only a _____ makes it.

4 painter, photographer, writer
They're all _____, but only a
_____ uses words.

5 dentist, doctor, nurse
They all _____ you, but only a
_____ looks at your teeth.

6 actor, dancer, singer
They all like to work on a _____,
but an _____ doesn't need music.

1 Read and answer.

Diggory Bones

1 What's Diggory's job? He's an archeologist.
2 Where does Brutus want Diggory to meet him? _____
3 Why did Diggory call him a "pirate"? _____
4 When are Diggory and Emily going to meet Brutus? _____
5 Is Brutus at the library? _____
6 Who has a letter for Diggory? _____

2 Read and order the text.

ancient languages. Brutus Grabbe took it from ☐

has the program, but he wants Diggory's ☐

The Baloney Stone is a very important computer 1

secret password. Brutus went on the evening news ☐

at the Old City Library at 10:45, but Brutus wasn't there. ☐

on TV to speak to Diggory. He told him to meet him ☐

program that can help us understand ☐

Diggory's classroom at the university. Now Brutus ☐

Do you remember?

1 A ____pilot____ flies planes.
2 A mechanic _____ cars.
3 When people have problems with their teeth, they see a _____ .
4 We use " _____ _____ " to talk and write about the future.
5 Two words that end in the /ər/ sound (as in "doctor") are _____ and _____ .
6 Two jobs that don't end in the /ər/ sound (as in "nurse") are _____ and _____ .

Can do

I can use *going to* to talk about the future.

I can talk about people at work.

I can write about different jobs.

How can we stay safe?

 Read and match.

SAFETY ON THE STREETS

It's important to stay safe on the streets, especially when riding a bike. Here are some safety tips:

1 Always wear
2 Make sure you use hand
3 Always ride
4 It's important to keep your bike
5 Always look out for

a signals when you slow down or turn a corner.
b in good condition.
c with lights at night.
d other vehicles on the streets.
e a helmet in case you have an accident.

FOLLOW THIS ADVICE AND STAY SAFE! — — —

 Plan to write a safety brochure. Complete the information about staying safe online.

Staying Safe Online

Dos

It's important to _____ .
Always _____ .
_____
_____
_____
_____

Don'ts

Don't _____ .
Never _____ .
_____
_____
_____
_____

 Use your notes to create a brochure about staying safe online.

 Did you ...

☐ plan your brochure?
☐ use imperatives?
☐ read your brochure again?
☐ check grammar, spelling, and punctuation?

Writing tip

We use imperatives when it's important to do something. Use imperatives with **always** and **never** to show what someone should and shouldn't do.

Always wear a helmet.

Never play with fire.

Social studies: safety procedures | critical thinking

Flyers Reading and Writing

1 **Read the letter and write the missing words. Write one word on each line.**

Dear KBTV,

Last Saturday, I saw something on your channel about a new quiz show for young people. It's _____called_____ **Boxing Brains**.

Example

I wrote to you last year about a different show, but you needed people who were older _____ me. I think this new quiz show is for children my age, and we have to _____ questions about different school subjects. I'm very _____ at geography and history, but science is my best subject.

1

2

3

I would like _____ go on the quiz show. Please can you send me _____ more information so that I can show my parents?

4

5

Regards,

Li Wei

1 **Read the story. Choose the words from the box to complete the sentences.**

> channel documentary firefighter going
> history jobs painted ~~show~~ quiz time

FRIENDLY

Friendly is a really funny comedy (1) _____show_____ . It's on TV at twenty to five every day. In this show, there are five friends who all go to the same school in a big city. They live and study in the school, but they aren't all in the same class.

They're all going to have different (2) _____ when they grow up. Peter wants to be a cook, Jenny wants to be an actor, Sally wants to be a taxi driver, Jim wants to be a (3) _____ , and Frankie wants to be an artist.

In last week's episode, Frankie (4) _____ a picture for an art competition, and Jenny sat as a model for her. In the picture that Frankie painted, Jenny had one square eye, which was red, and a carrot for a nose. One of her legs was a cell phone, and the other was a banana. Frankie's friends don't think she's (5) _____ to win the competition, but Frankie's happy with her painting. She knows that she'll be a famous artist one day!

2 **Choose a title for this episode of *Friendly*.**

a Modern art

b Fun and games

c Beautiful people

3 **Draw and color Frankie's painting.**

4 **Match the questions to the answers.**

1 Why do zebras like old movies?

2 What goes up slowly and comes down quickly?

3 What do you call bears with no ears?

4 What's always slow to come, but never arrives?

5 When do elephants have eight feet?

☐	When there are two of them!
☐	B.
1	Because they're in black and white.
☐	An elephant in an elevator.
☐	Tomorrow.

5 **Complete the sentences. Count and write the letters.**

1 The winner of the competition gets a
   _____prize_____ . [5]

2 The study of the past is called
   _____ . ☐

3 Eight fifteen is _____
   after eight. ☐

4 We draw and paint in this class.
   _____ ☐

5 Good, better, _____ . ☐

6 The study of different countries
   is called _____ . ☐

7 A competition with questions is a
   _____ show. ☐

8 Somebody who repairs cars is a
   _____ . ☐

9 Something we study at school is called
   a _____ . ☐

10 A manager uses this machine in an office.
   It's called a _____ . ☐

11 Eleven thirty is _____
   past eleven. ☐

12 Soccer and basketball are
   _____ . ☐

13 Somebody who paints pictures is
   an _____ . ☐

14 The opposite of "work" is _____ . ☐

6 **Now complete the crossword. Write the message.**

			p	r	i	z	²e

1	2	3	3	4		5	1	2	6	2
	e							e		e

7 **Quiz time!**

1 What languages can they study at City School? They can study _____

2 In which class do we learn about plants and the human body?

3 How can we film animals from the air?

4 What does Sally think she's going to be?

5 What jobs did George Orwell have?

6 What can we use to cover the flames of a fire?

8 **Write questions for your quiz in your notebook.**

STUDY AGAIN | Directions

right ⌐► left ◄⌐ straight ahead ⇈ corner ◄⌐ past □↑ across ⇮ straight down ⟵

★1 Read and answer the questions.

Yesterday afternoon, five people got on a bus at the bus station: one man, two women, and two children. The bus left the station at nine o'clock. It had to stop at the corner because the traffic lights were red. The bus turned left after the traffic lights.

The bus didn't stop at the first bus stop, but drove straight ahead because there weren't any people waiting there and no one wanted to get off. The bus turned right at the next corner and drove over the bridge. At the second bus stop, outside the school, the two children and the man got off, and nine more people got on. Then the bus went into the train station, where ten people got off and 12 more got on. The bus drove out of the station, turned left, and went straight ahead to the end of the street.

1 How many people got off at the second stop?

_____

2 How many times did the bus turn left?

_____

3 How many people were there on the bus when it drove out of the train station?

_____

★2 Mark ✓ or ✗ for each sentence.

1 Yesterday morning, six people got on a bus at the bus station: two men, one woman, and three children. _____

2 The bus had to stop at the corner because the traffic lights were red. _____

3 After the first bus stop, it turned left at the next corner. _____

4 At the second bus stop, outside the hospital, the two children and the man got off. _____

★3 Read and complete the sentences.

~~across~~ left on the corner right
straight ahead straight down

1 She ran ____across____ the park.

2 She turned _____ at the corner of Elm Street.

3 He went _____ at the traffic lights.

4 He waited for his friend _____ outside the school.

5 She turned _____ onto Oak Street.

6 He walked _____ Cherry Street.

Do the online activities on **Practice Extra** as you complete this unit.

1 Follow the directions and write the message.

London	to	29	places	million	is
of	see,	the	interesting	in	and
a lot	are	year	visit	people	every
biggest	There	U.K.	it.	city	the

r = right   l = left   u = up   d = down

London – 5r – 3d – 5l – 4r – 2u – 2l – 2d – 1l – 1u – 1l – 1u – 3r – 1u – 2l – 1d – 4r – 1d – 3l – 2u – 2r – 2d – 1l – 1d

London   is   the _____ _____ _____

_____ _____ _____ _____ _____ _____

_____ _____ _____ _____ _____ _____

2 Label these buildings on the map.

1 The gym's on the right of the supermarket.
2 The movie theater's across from the bus station.
3 The castle's across from the parking lot.
4 The library's between the café and the toy store.
5 The school's on the other side of the street from the bookstore and across from the hospital.
6 The bookstore's behind the fire station.
7 The stadium's on the other side of the street from the bookstore, on the corner.

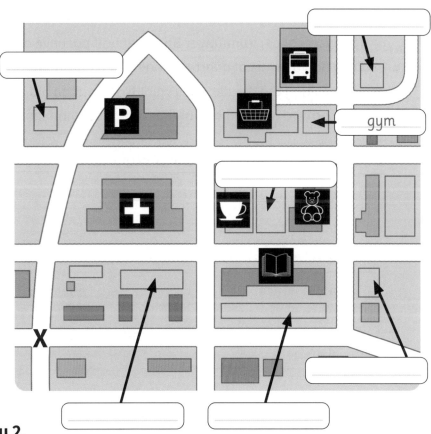

3 Find these buildings in Activity 2.

1 Start at the X. Go straight ahead and take the first street on the right. Go past the hospital and the café. It's the building on the left, before the toy store. What is it? _____
2 Start at the X. Turn right and walk to the fire station. Go past the fire station and walk to the next corner. Turn left. It's on the corner on the right. What is it? _____

4 Now write two sets of directions for a partner to follow in your notebook.

1 Look and complete the words.

1 h o t e l

2 r _ _ t _ _ r _ _ t

3 m _ _ v _ e t h _ _ _ t _ _

4 p _ l _ _ st _ t _ _ _

5 c _ _ _ l _

6 a _ _ p _ _ _ _

2 Complete the table. Look in the Student's Book to find the names of the places.

Yesterday Yuna visited London with her family.

- At nine o'clock, Yuna went to a place where you can see exciting things from all over the world.
- They went for a boat trip on the River Thames at ten thirty.
- After lunch, they went to the place where Shakespeare and his actors showed their plays.
- They took a taxi from Tower Bridge at half past five and went back to their hotel.
- They had a picnic at quarter to one. They ate some sandwiches in Hyde Park.
- After visiting the theater, they went to look at an old building next to Tower Bridge.
- They arrived at their hotel at ten to six. They had dinner and went to bed.

9:00	Went to the British Museum.
10:30	
2:30	
4:30	
5:50	

3 Look at the letters on the clock and write the words.

1 It's five to one.   straight

2 It's eight o'clock.   _____

3 It's ten to six.   _____

4 It's ten after nine.   _____

5 It's twenty-five after four. _____

6 It's twenty-five to three.   _____

sch
stra   ight
st   p
ark   eet
ool   ore
str   st
adium

Write "who," "that," or "where."

1 A place ____where____ you can mail letters and postcards.

2 Someone _____ flies planes.

3 Something _____ you have to buy when you travel by bus or train.

4 A place _____ we go to see a play.

5 Someone _____ cooks food in a restaurant.

6 A place _____ you can see old paintings and books.

7 A place _____ you can catch a plane.

8 A place _____ you can get money.

9 Someone _____ repairs cars.

10 A place _____ you go to cross a river.

 Now find the words from Activity 1.

a	c	e	t	u	r	e	d	p	m
i	q	p	i	l	o	t	b	m	u
r	c	y	c	s	z	a	r	e	s
p	o	s	t	o	f	f	i	c	e
o	b	p	h	d	o	v	d	h	u
r	a	a	e	u	l	k	g	a	m
t	n	k	a	o	a	n	e	n	y
c	k	w	t	k	r	o	t	i	p
f	t	b	e	t	p	i	e	c	o
s	u	c	r	t	i	c	k	e	t

 Write a definition for these words.

1 A place _____

2 Someone _____

 Label these places on your map.

> airport   bank   ~~castle~~   hotel
> museum   restaurant   theater

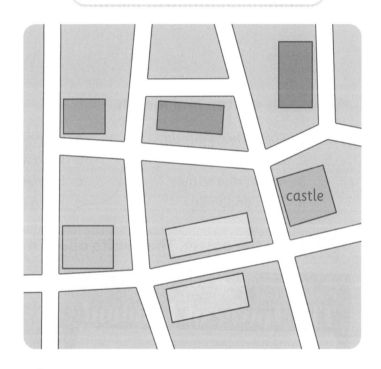

castle

 Now write directions from the castle to three places on the map.

1 Start at the castle. Go ...

Ask a partner to follow your directions.

Sounds and life skills
Choosing options

Pronunciation focus

1 🎧 10 **Match to make words. Listen and check.**

1	st	-orts stadium
2	str	-ool
3	sp	-ore
4	sky	-are
5	sch	-scraper
6	squ	-eet

2 🎧 11 **Listen and circle.**

1 What time does the
sports stadium / (swimming pool) open?

2 Why don't we visit the museum at the top of the
skyscraper / store?

3 Look at the map and go straight ahead, up the
stairs / street.

4 You don't have to **stand / study** at the
school / sports stadium.

5 Let's go **skating / skateboarding** down that
stream / street.

3 🎧 12 **Listen and match.**

1 The British Museum   a is a special way to travel in a big city.
2 Tower Bridge   b is exciting and fun, with amazing views.
3 A boat on the river   c is a great place to take pictures.
4 The London Eye   d has a lot of interesting things to see inside.

4 **Read the poster. Then write about a place to visit in your town or city.**

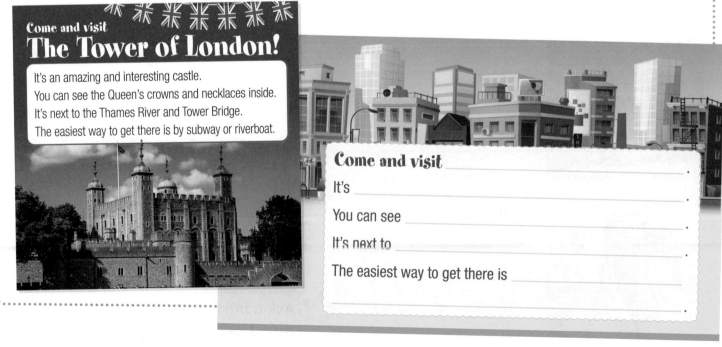

Come and visit
The Tower of London!

It's an amazing and interesting castle.
You can see the Queen's crowns and necklaces inside.
It's next to the Thames River and Tower Bridge.
The easiest way to get there is by subway or riverboat.

Come and visit _____
It's _____
You can see _____
It's next to _____
The easiest way to get there is _____

1 Read and answer.

Diggory Bones

1 Why was it the wrong library? Because it was the wrong city.
2 Which city does Brutus mean? _____
3 What are they going to do now? _____
4 What is there outside Alexandria? _____
5 What's on the walls of the cave? _____
6 Who's the taxi driver? _____

2 Who said it? Read and match.

a I think he means the city of Alexandria in Egypt. ☐ 1

b Brutus can use the Baloney Stone to understand the writing! ☐

c What are we going to do now? ☐

d … can open the door to mountains of secret treasure! ☐

e Now let's get a cab and find a hotel. ☐

f Yes, son. ☐

Do you remember?

1 An actor often works in a _____theater_____ .
2 You can stay in a _____ when you go on vacation.
3 Be careful when you walk _____ the street. Look out for cars!
4 The opposite of "turn right" is "turn _____."
5 Two words with "st" (as in "<u>st</u>ation") are _____ and _____ .
6 Two words with "sp" (as in "<u>sp</u>orts") are _____ and _____ .

Can do

I can talk about places around town.

I can give and understand directions.

I can write directions to places around town.

What are the best modes of transportation?

1 Read and circle.

Quick and Easy Transportation

One of the (1) **more good** / **best** ways to travel around the busy cities of Vietnam is by rickshaw. You can travel (2) **faster** / **fastest** than by taxi this way, and the rickshaw is also the (3) **more** / **most** eco-friendly way to travel these days. It doesn't need fuel, so it's (4) **better** / **best** for the environment than cars. Rickshaws are bicycles with a seat in the front for passengers. The driver sits behind. It can only take one or two passengers, but it's definitely (5) **quicker** / **quickest** than a taxi!

2 Plan to write an ad. Complete the information about a mode of transportation.

Mode of Transportation: _____

Get people interested:

If you don't have a car, why don't you

_____.

What are the advantages?

They're faster / cheaper / better than

_____

because _____.

The _____ is the fastest / cheapest / best mode of transportation in the world!

You can _____.

3 Use your notes to create an ad for the transportation.

4 Did you …

- ☐ plan your ad?
- ☐ use comparatives and superlatives?
- ☐ read your ad again?
- ☐ check grammar, spelling, and punctuation?

Writing tip

We use comparatives to talk about two things.

Trains are **faster than** buses in my city.

We use superlatives to talk about one thing from a group of similar things.

Buses are **the cheapest** way to travel in my city.

You can use comparatives and superlatives in your ad to say why your transportation is the best.

Geography: city life | 🛡 critical thinking

Flyers Listening

1 🎧 **13** **Listen and write. There is one example.**

BRISTOL → LONDON
9:00 – 1·SEPT·22
39A

George's vacation in London

Transportation:	by _____train_____	
1 Hotel name:	The _____	
2 Where the hotel is:	next to the British _____	
3 Hotel phone number:	_____	
4 Where George visited:	The _____ Theater	
5 Time of the play:	Sunday at _____	

4 Disaster!

We use the past progressive to describe what was happening in the past.

Affirmative	Negative (n't = not)	Question
I **was listening** to music.	You **weren't playing** tennis.	**Was** she **reading**?
They **were walking** to school.	He **wasn't running** in the park.	**Were** they **sailing**?

 Match the pictures to the text.

Emma's talking to her teacher. She's saying why she was late for school.

☐ Then I saw the bus. It was coming down the street, so I started to run.

☐ The books were in the street in the water when the bus ran over them.

☐ I didn't have a coat or umbrella, so I decided to catch the bus.

☐ Now I can't find my homework. It must be in the street. Sorry! And I'm sorry I'm late!

☐1 I had a disaster this morning. I was walking to school when it started to rain.

☐ When I was running for the bus, I dropped my backpack and my books fell out into the street.

 Write the verbs in the table. Look at the spelling.

carry   cook   cut   enjoy   get   live   lose   ~~move~~   shout   stop   swim   wake up

taking (e + -ing)	sailing (+ -ing)	running (x2 + -ing)
moving		

 Read and choose the right words.

1 They were sailing across the lake (when) / **because** it started to rain.
2 He was **climb** / **climbing** in the mountains when it started to snow.
3 My dad was taking a shower when the phone **ring** / **rang**.
4 The boy **was** / **were** flying his kite when he hurt his elbow.
5 They were losing **if** / **when** he scored the goal.

Do the online activities on Practice Extra as you complete this unit.

1 Write questions and answers about Akash's day.

1 What was Akash doing at twenty after three?   He was catching the bus.

2 _____

3 _____

4 _____

5 _____

6 _____

2 Read and complete the table.

Last week, someone broke a chair in the classroom during playtime. The children don't want to tell the teacher who broke the chair, so the teacher is trying to find out.

Oliver was wearing a red sweater and a long scarf. Freya was wearing a short skirt and green shoes. Katy was wearing jeans and a T-shirt. Kito was wearing gray pants and a blue shirt.

The girl wearing jeans was jumping around the classroom. The boy wearing a blue shirt was playing soccer outside. One girl was reading a book on the playground. Oliver was talking to his friends on the playground. The child who broke the chair wasn't wearing green shoes or gray pants.

Name	Oliver			
Clothes				
Where?				
What doing?				

Who broke the chair? _____

1 Choose the dates from the box to label the pictures.

> April 14, 1912   August 26, 1883   December 28, 1908
> May 6, 1937   ~~November 1, 1755~~   October 10–16, 1780

November 1, 1755 _____   _____   _____   _____   _____

2 Read and write the dates.

1 The day before the twenty-fifth.
The twenty-fourth

2 The day after the twenty-first.

_____

3 The day after the twenty-fourth.

_____

4 This day is three days after the twenty-sixth.

_____

5 This is the day after the twenty-second.

_____

6 This day is three days before the thirtieth.

_____

3 Complete the sentences.

1 The first month is
January .

2 The third month is
_____ .

3 The fifth month is
_____ .

4 The seventh month is
_____ .

5 The eleventh month is
_____ .

6 The twelfth month is
_____ .

4 Look and complete the months. Put them in order.

A _____

J ___ e

S _____

O _____

M _____

D _____

M _____

J _____

1 | J a n u a r y

A _____

N _____

F _____

1 Answer the questions.

1 What date was it yesterday? It was _____

2 What date is it going to be next Saturday? _____

3 When's your birthday? _____

4 When's your friend's birthday? _____

5 When's your teacher's birthday? _____

6 What date does school end this year? _____

 2 Match the words to the pictures.

1 storm   2 tsunami   3 ice   4 hurricane

5 volcano   6 fog   7 fire   8 lightning

  1

 3 Now match the words and pictures to the definitions.

a Heavy rain and strong winds. [1]

b Very cold water that is solid, not liquid. ☐

c A mountain with a big hole at the top through which liquid rock and hot gas can come out. ☐

d Electricity in the air that passes from one cloud to another or to the ground. ☐

e Burning material and gases that can burn other things. ☐

f A cloud that is near the ground or the ocean. ☐

g An enormous and fast wave. ☐

h This is the worst kind of storm, with very strong winds and heavy rain. ☐

Sounds and life skills
Thinking creatively
Pronunciation focus

1 🎧 14 **Follow the /eɪ/ sounds. Listen and check.**

wave	train	Sarah	glass	lazy	straight	lake
cab	station	diary	parrot	safe	carrot	highway
map	April	break	bank	waiter	camel	dangerous
jam	August	rainbow	land	name	math	brave
airport	farm	email	today	Katy	path	thank

2 🎧 15 **Write the words next to their vowel sounds. Listen and check.**

> ~~cheap~~ do dry feet food gray glue ~~hole~~ ~~ice~~ kind knee
> light ~~May~~ please rain ~~shoes~~ skate snow toe throw

A /eɪ/ _____ May _____

E /i/ _____ cheap _____

I /aɪ/ _____ ice _____

O /oʊ/ _____ hole _____

U /u/ _____ shoes _____

3 🎧 16 **Use the words from Activity 2 to complete the rhymes. Listen and check.**

1 Why didn't you fly your kite today?
Because it was cloudy, and the sky
was ___ gray ___ .

2 It's sunny and windy. Can I fly my kite?
Yes, get the blue one! It's nice and
_____ .

3 Why didn't you go out and play in the snow?
Because yesterday I fell and hurt my
_____ .

4 We can't find the glue! We can't find the glue!
We broke Mom's cup! What should we
_____ ?

4 **Read, look, and answer. Your words don't have to rhyme.**

1 Why didn't you swim in the ocean?
_____

2 Why didn't you bake your friend a cake?
_____

3 Why didn't you go to the amusement park?
_____

1 Read and answer.

Diggory Bones

1 What does "Canis Major" mean? It means "the big dog."
2 What's the brightest star called? _____
3 What was the date in the story? _____
4 When did Diggory remember the disaster? _____
5 What destroyed ancient Alexandria? _____
6 What came after the volcanic eruption? _____

2 Complete the sentences from the story. Match them to the pictures.

~~date~~   dangerous   hot   light   secret   storm

1 What's the ___date___ today, Emily?
2 Night's falling, and a _____'s coming.
3 Is it too _____ for you, Bones?
4 Today it's going to show us the "opening" of the _____ cave!
5 It's really _____ down here.
6 Run to the _____, Emily!

Do you remember?

1 It's very difficult to see when the weather is ___foggy___ .
2 We sometimes see _____ in the sky when there's a storm.
3 Today's date in numbers is _____ .
4 Tomorrow's date in words is _____ .
5 Two words the /oʊ/ sound are _____ and _____ .
6 Two words with the /u/ sound are _____ and _____ .

Can do

I can talk about the weather and disasters.

I can talk about things that were happening in the past.

I can write a story.

Where can we find volcanoes?

1 **Read and match.**

1 During summer vacation, I visited Santa María del Oro,

2 It's on a dormant volcano,

3 There are pools of thermal water around the lake,

4 You can eat in one of the restaurants,

a which often serve fresh fish from the lake.

b which is a town in the state of Nayarit in Mexico.

c which people swim in because it's healthy.

d which is famous for its beautiful lake in the crater.

2 **Plan to write an email. Complete the information about a famous place you visited.**

Who are you writing to?

Where did you go?

What's it famous for?

What can you see / do there?

Would you like to go back? Why?

Ending

Hi _____,

During summer vacation, I visited _____.

_____ is a _____ in _____,

which is famous for its _____.

In _____, you can see _____,

which _____.

There are also _____.

I hope I can go back to / you can visit _____ one day

because it's _____.

See you soon,

_____

3 **Use your notes to write an email to a partner about the place.**

4 **Did you ...**
- [ ] plan your email?
- [ ] use *which* to give extra information?
- [ ] start and end your email correctly?
- [ ] read your email again?
- [ ] check grammar, spelling, and punctuation?

Writing tip

We can use *which* to give extra information. You can use it to make your writing more interesting.

Edinburgh is a city in Scotland, **which is famous for its old castle.**

Geography and history: natural landscapes | critical thinking

Flyers Reading and Writing

1 Emma's talking to her friend David about what he did last night. What does David say to Emma?

Read the conversation and choose the best answer.
Write a letter (A–E) for each answer.
There is one example.

Example

Emma: Did you watch TV last night?

David: _____ D _____

Questions

1  **Emma:** What did you watch?

David: _____

2  **Emma:** What was it about?

David: _____

3  **Emma:** Really, was there anything on earthquakes?

David: _____

4  **Emma:** What time did it finish?

David: _____

A Yes, there was. It was really amazing.
B I watched a documentary.
C It wasn't late. It finished at seven o'clock.
D Yes, I did. **(Example)**
E It was all about natural disasters.

1 Read the story. Choose the words from the box to complete the sentences.

> corner   left   ~~March~~   movie theater   quarter
> restaurant   right   straight   walking   wasn't   were

FRIENDLY

Last Saturday, (1)_____March_____ 30, was Jim's birthday. He decided to go to downtown with Peter to have lunch in an expensive (2)_____ and to go to the movies. They went to the station at (3)_____ after nine on Saturday morning and caught the train from platform I. They didn't know the city very well, and they didn't have a map, so they decided to explore. When they were walking down a long street, they turned (4)_____, not right, and got lost. When they were trying to find the right street, they saw hotels, post offices, gyms, and museums, but no restaurants. At ten after two, they found a small café. They were really hungry, so they stopped there and had a burger and fries for lunch. When they got to the movie theater, they found it (5)_____ showing the action movie they wanted to see – it was showing a cartoon about funny animals for very young children.

They were (6)_____ back to the station when it started to rain heavily, and they didn't have any coats. Jim thought that his birthday was the biggest disaster ever, but then Peter started to laugh loudly and they agreed it was the funniest birthday ever.

 2 Choose a title for this episode of *Friendly*.

a The best day   b The wrong map   c What a disaster!

 3 Find the one that is not like the others and write why.

1 across   next to   (museum)   behind
   Museum – because it's a building.

2 hotel   taxi   restaurant   theater
   _____

3 stadium   left   between   right
   _____

4 rainbow   rain   snow   tsunami
   _____

5 sailed   ran   flew   help
   _____

6 February   Thursday   April   October
   _____

4 Complete the sentences. Count and write the letters.

1 This is another word for a road. It's a ___street___ . [6]

2 The lightning _____ their boat. [ ]

3 The opposite of "inside" is _____ . [ ]

4 The tenth month is _____ . [ ]

5 There was a forest _____ last summer. It burned everything. [ ]

6 The place where we go to catch a plane is an _____ . [ ]

7 Clouds on the ground are called _____ . [ ]

8 The month that comes before September is _____ . [ ]

9 There's a _____ when there's heavy rain and a strong wind. [ ]

10 We go to a _____ to see sculptures and paintings. [ ]

11 We use a _____ to help us find our way. [ ]

12 The point where two streets meet is a _____ . [ ]

13 We need a _____ to walk across a river. [ ]

14 The first month is _____ . [ ]

5 Now complete the crossword. Write the message.

1	2	3	5	8	9	6	2		5	6	4	5	7
s														!

6 Quiz time!

1 What's the name of the busiest airport in the U.K.? The busiest airport is _____

2 When was the cable car system in Medellín built? _____

3 What was Sally's dad listening to on the boat? _____

4 What do we call dangerous storms with strong winds? _____

5 Where are more than 75% of the Earth's volcanoes? _____

7 Write questions for your quiz in your notebook.

5 Material things

We use *made of* to describe materials.

Affirmative	Negative (n't = not)	Question
It's **made of** chocolate.	It isn't **made of** paper.	Is it **made of** sugar?
They're **made of** stone.	They aren't **made of** wood.	Are they **made of** leaves?

 Match the words to the pictures.

~~bone~~ bricks grass leaves paper stone

bone

 Read and order the words.

1 made / This / is / jacket / fur. / of
This jacket is made of fur.

2 isn't / skirt / That / made / chocolate. / of
_____

3 your / of? / sweater / made / What's
_____

4 T-shirt / your / Is / of / made / fur?
_____

5 made / of / their / shoes / Are / wood?
_____

6 paper. / clothes / made / are / of / His
_____

 Correct the sentences.

1 My hats is made of fur.
2 The spider has made of paper.
3 The cake aren't made of chocolate.
4 Is his jacket made off rubber?
5 Are their houses mades of stone?
6 My book is make of paper.

 What are they made of?
Look and write.

They're made of chocolate.

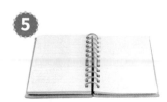 

1 **Write the correct sentences.**

Our house	made	of paper.
The boat is	is made	of rubber.
My book's	are made	of stone.
Their tires	made of	wood.

1 _____
2 _____
3 _____
4 _____

 2 **Read, look, and label the picture.**

My house is made of wood, and it has grass on the roof. Grass is really good because it's very green. The house stays hot in the winter and cold in the summer. When it snows, I can ski on it!

The door is made of wood. The windows are made of water bottles. When it rains, the water from the roof goes into the window bottles. I use it to water my plants. There are leaves over the balcony. I can sit under them when it's sunny.

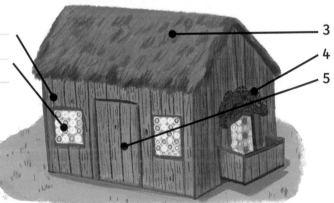

1 house made of wood
2 _____
3 _____
4 _____
5 _____

 3 **Read and complete the text.** bottles bridges gold ~~materials~~ stone thousand

The Romans were the first people to use a lot of different
(1) _____materials_____ , both for building and in their everyday life.
They were very good at making things from a lot of different metals,
including (2) _____ and silver.

They made a lot of things with glass, like (3) _____ and
glasses for drinking.

The Romans made houses from wood, (4) _____ , and
concrete. They also built 50,000 kilometers of roads and were the first
people to be really good at making (5) _____ .

The first bridge with a name was the Pons Fabricius, and it was made
of stone. They built it over the River Tiber in Rome in 62 BCE, and it's
there today, two (6) _____ years later.

Choose the words from the box to label the pictures.

cardboard   ~~glass~~   gold   metal   paper   plastic   silver   wood   wool

glass   ___   ___   ___   ___   ___

 Find and write eight materials.

p	a	p	e	r	y	w	u	a	p
l	s	c	o	s	i	l	v	e	r
a	k	t	a	m	a	t	l	c	b
s	a	o	d	r	f	e	q	o	w
t	w	t	n	f	d	a	i	l	o
i	g	o	l	d	u	a	h	t	o
c	n	m	o	v	m	e	t	a	l
d	c	p	o	d	g	l	a	s	s

1 g o l d
2 s _____
3 p _____
4 w ___ d
5 g _____ s
6 p _____
7 m _____
8 w ___ l

Write the words.

1 A man-made material. We make it from oil.
    plastic

2 An expensive white metal. _____

3 Animal hair. _____

4 Windows are made of this. It can break easily.

    _____

5 We get this material from sheep.

    _____

6 An expensive yellow metal. _____

7 The material we write on in our notebooks.

    _____

8 This material is made from wood. It's thicker
    than paper. _____

Look at the letters on the clock and write the words.

1 It's twenty-five after twelve.   gold
2 It's ten to three.   _____
3 It's twenty to two.   _____
4 It's half past four.   _____
5 It's quarter to eleven.   _____
6 It's twenty-five to one.   _____

ld
ver   er
wo   ss
sil   od
gla   tal
pap   go
me

1 Read. Change one letter to write a new word.

face	Part of our body, on the front of our head.
race	A competition to see who's the fastest.
	Something we eat.
	Good, kind.
	A number between eight and ten.
	My things, something I have.
	A straight mark on a page or drawing.
	The opposite of "don't like."
	Where do you … ?
	The opposite of "hate."
	We do this with our body when we dance.
	Gold is … expensive than silver.
	The past of "wear."
	The opposite of "play."
	Part of a sentence.
	We get this material from trees.
	We get this material from sheep.
pool	Somewhere we can go to swim.

2 Now write the clues for this puzzle.

well	The opposite of "badly."
wall	
ball	
tall	
talk	
walk	

3 Find eight mistakes in the text.

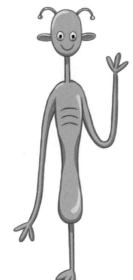

Glook's from a different world. He's doing a project about Earth, and there are a lot of mistakes. Can you help him correct his homework?

People on Earth use things that are made of different materials. Plastic, wood, and (dictionaries) are all different materials. Bottles are made of glass or paper. Tables and chairs can be made of fog, clouds, or metal. People on Earth like reading books, comic books, and volcanoes. These are made of paper and wool. Earth people get wool from parrots. I'm going to visit Earth next November. I want to get a nice big bracelet made of water. I can wear it when I go to parties.

4 Now write the text correctly.

People on Earth use things that are made of different materials. Plastic, wood, and cardboard are all different materials.

Sounds and life skills
Talking about different ideas
Pronunciation focus

1 🎧 17 **Listen and complete.**

1 ___Look at___ this!
Wow! That's amazing!

2 _____!
I'm coming!

3 _____!
Ouch!

4 I have _____ great _____!
What is it?

5 _____ star!
I know!

2 🎧 18 **Look and match. Then listen and circle the connected letters.**

1 chocola(te e)ggs
2 two glass eyes
3 purple ice cream
4 a lot of red apples
5 an insect made of sugar

3 🎧 19 **Choose a phrase from Activity 1. Listen and check.**

4 **Complete the comic strip. Add speech bubbles using phrases from Activity 1.**

1 Look at this!

2 _____

3 _____
Nice!

4 _____

Two friends go to a fair.
Look! There's a fair!
Let's go and see!

They visit a joke tent with a lot of fun things to look at.

One friend scares the other with a joke.

And then …

1 Read and answer.

Diggory Bones

1 What was Brutus carrying in his bag? He was carrying the Baloney Stone.
2 What's the inside of Brutus's bag made of? _____
3 What did Brutus push? _____
4 Why's it dangerous to joke about Sirius? _____
5 What are the bowls made of? _____
6 What does Brutus want? _____

2 Read and order the text.

in his bag, but the Baloney Stone's safe ☐

because the inside's made of plastic. Diggory ☐

Brutus is carrying the computer 1

the instructions. Brutus pushes the picture ☐

Cleopatra's treasure from her underwater palace. ☐

of the snake, and a secret door opens. They ☐

find a lot of treasure behind the wall. It's ☐

understands the writing on the wall and reads ☐

Do you remember?

1 Furniture is often made of _____ wood _____ .
2 Scarves are made of _____ .
3 Gold and silver are precious _____ .
4 My friend is afraid _____ spiders.
5 Complete the phrase: "You're a _____ ."
6 Complete the phrase: "Wait a _____ ."

Can do

I can talk about materials.

I can talk about what things are made of.

I can write a description of my classroom.

What can you make with recycled materials?

1 **Read and circle the adverbs.**

The Singing Ringing Tree

This sculpture is called *The Singing Tree*. I saw it in England when I was on vacation. It's (really) interesting because it's a sculpture, but it sings, too!

It's made of metal pipes in the shape of a tree. It's an amazing sculpture because the sun shines brightly on the pipes. When the wind blows gently through the pipes, we can hear beautiful music.

I love the idea because the sculpture shows nature and the wind makes it alive. When I hear the sculpture sing, I'm completely relaxed. It's a smart idea to mix man-made materials with nature.

2 **Plan to write a review. Complete the information about an interesting sculpture.**

Name of sculpture	It's called _____.
Where is it?	I saw the sculpture _____.
What materials does it use?	The sculpture is made of _____.
	There is / are _____.
What's interesting or different about it?	It's interesting / different because _____.
	_____ is my favorite because _____.
	I love the way the artist _____.
What idea does the sculpture show?	The sculpture shows _____.

3 **Use your notes to write a review of the sculpture.**

4 **Did you ...**

- ☐ plan your review?
- ☐ use adverbs?
- ☐ read your review again?
- ☐ check grammar, spelling, and punctuation?

Writing tip

We use adverbs to describe how we do something.

> I love the way the artist **skilfully** joined all the objects together.

We can also use them to make our ideas and feelings stronger.

> When I hear the sculpture sing, I'm **completely** relaxed.

Flyers Listening

1 🎧 20 **Whose things are these?**

Listen and write a letter in each box. There is one example.

 Sarah [E]　 Robert ☐　 Emma ☐　 Richard ☐　 Katy ☐　 Michael ☐

A

B

C

D

E

F

6 Senses

We use verb + *like* to describe things.

Affirmative	Negative (n't = not)	Question
It **looks like** a ball.	It **doesn't sound like** a car.	**What** does it **feel like**?
It **smells like** a lemon.	It **doesn't taste like** chocolate.	**What** does it **look like**?

 1 Read and order the words.

1 blue cheese / smells / That / old / terrible.
That old blue cheese smells terrible.

2 it's / rain. / going to / It / looks / like

_____

3 smartphone. / That / like / your / sounds

_____

4 like? / does / this / toy mouse / What / feel

_____

5 Her / cake / coffee. / tastes / like

_____

6 look / like? / What / my picture / does

_____

 2 Correct the sentences.

1 Your smartphone sound ^s like a frog.
2 My sweater doesn't feels like fur.
3 That pen look likes a banana.

4 This cookie don't taste like chocolate.
5 What does that cheese smells like?
6 I doesn't look like my dad.

 3 Read and complete the email.

exciting   feel   felt   hear   quickly   ~~Saturday~~   shouting

Hi Frank,

How was your weekend? I had a really good one because on (1) _Saturday_ we went to a new amusement park. It's really (2) _____ and has a lot of things to do. Can you see the picture of the rollercoaster? It's amazing!
That's me (3) _____ loudly. I thought it looked dangerous, but I didn't (4) _____ afraid. It was very loud, though – I couldn't (5) _____ anything.

I also went on a big wheel. You sit in a chair, and it goes around and around very (6) _____ . At first I felt excited, but then I felt sick. When I got off, I still (7) _____ dizzy for a while, so I'm not going on that wheel again!

Let's talk soon.

Richard

Do the online activities on Practice Extra as you complete this unit.

How do they look? Write the answers.

1 She looks happy.

2 _____

3 _____

4 _____

5 _____

6 _____

 Read. What are they?

1 It looks like an apple, but it isn't round. It's green or yellow. What is it? _a pear_

2 It looks like a bean, but it isn't. It's green, small, and round. What is it? _____

3 It's a fruit, and it tastes like a lime, but it isn't green. It's yellow. What is it? _____

4 It's a hot drink. Some people have it with sugar and milk. It sometimes looks like coffee, but it doesn't taste like coffee. What is it? _____

5 They sometimes taste like burgers. They're long and thin. What are they? _____

6 This sounds like a lion, but it isn't. It has orange fur and black stripes. What is it? _____

 Read and answer the sense quiz questions.

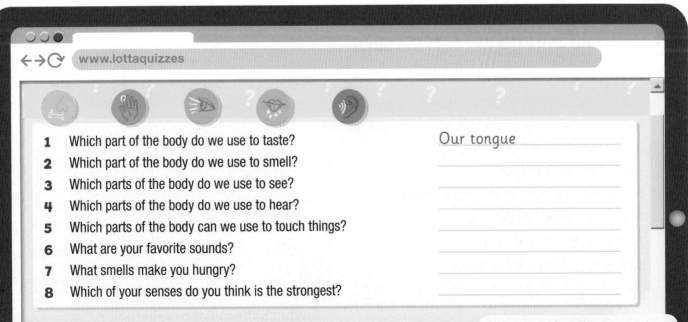

www.lottaquizzes

1 Which part of the body do we use to taste? _Our tongue_

2 Which part of the body do we use to smell?

3 Which parts of the body do we use to see?

4 Which parts of the body do we use to hear?

5 Which parts of the body can we use to touch things?

6 What are your favorite sounds?

7 What smells make you hungry?

8 Which of your senses do you think is the strongest?

Language: describing sensations

Look and complete the words.

p e p p e r

 s _ _ t

 k n _ _ _ _

 f _ _ k

 s p _ _ _ _

p _ _ t

 **Find the words and answer the questions.**

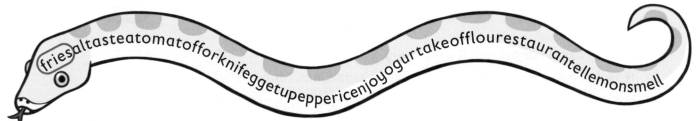

There are 20 words.

Nine are food words. What are they? fries, _____

Seven are verbs (two have two words). What are they? _____

Two are things we eat with. What are they? _____

One is a preposition. What is it? _____

One is somewhere we go to eat. What is it? _____

 Read and write the words in the puzzle.

1 We put this on our food. It's black or white. _____ pepper _____

2 We use this with a knife when we eat. _____

3 We use this in cooking. It's white. We get it from the ocean or the ground. _____

4 Famous Italian food. _____

5 We put our food on this when we eat. _____

6 Bread is made of this. _____

7 We use this to cut meat. _____

8 We use this to eat ice cream. _____

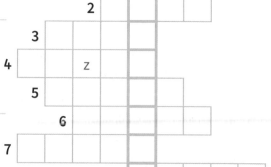

What's the mystery vegetable? _____

Read and complete the text.

> 900   cook   cheese   flour   Italy   largest
> made   meals   meters   ~~people~~   pizzas   taste   top

The (1) ___people___ from Naples (Napoli) in (2) _____

were the first to make (3) _____. Their pizzas were

(4) _____ of a bread base, with (5) _____, tomato,

and olives on top. Pizza is one of the most popular (6) _____ in

the world, not only in Italy, because it's (7) _____ delicious.

Some pizzas can have extra things on (8) _____.

They can have thicker bases, and sometimes the (9) _____

can fold the pizza in half and fill it with more cheese and things. They cook pizzas in an oven.

The (10) _____ pizza ever made was in South Africa in 1990. It was enormous! It was 37.4

(11) _____ across and was made with 500 kg of (12) _____, 800 kg of cheese, and

(13) _____ kg of tomatoes. Amazing!

 Read and order the text.

	shows. When his family came home, it looked like the kitchen was on
	were out. He decided to cook sausages and potatoes. He turned on the
1	Tom's 14. Last Saturday he decided to make lunch for his family while they
	into the hot water. He did that because sugar looks like salt and he didn't read
6	the label on the box. Then he went into the living room to watch TV while he
	to turn on the clock. Then he started to cook the potatoes, but he put sugar
	was waiting for the food to cook, and started to watch one of his favorite
9	fire. When they opened the oven, the sausages looked small and black. The
	potatoes were OK, but they tasted sweet. Tom's mom said he invented sweet potatoes!
	oven, and when it felt hot, he put the sausages in it, but he forgot

Sounds and life skills
Describing sensations
Pronunciation focus

1 🎧 **21** **Listen and circle the stressed words.**

1 hot chocolate (blue cheese) sandwiches cake
2 fruit pineapple schoolbag lunchbox

3 Sam Suzie stomachache swimming
4 guitar piano class school

2 🎧 **22** **Listen again and complete.**

1 I don't like ____blue____ ____cheese____ in my _____ !
2 _____ taking _____ in my _____ !
3 _____ well. She's _____ .
4 I'm _____ .

3 🎧 **23** **Listen and complete.**

My ____birthday____ !
It looks like colorful _____ and candles.
It tastes like birthday _____ .
It smells like _____ after I blow them out.
It sounds like my _____ laughing and having _____ .
It feels like a _____ from my _____ .

4 **Look at the pictures and write.**

It feels like …   It looks like …   It sounds like …
It smells like …   It tastes like …

 _____

 _____

 _____

 _____

 _____

1 Read and answer.

1 Where does Brutus fall? <u>He falls into a snake bowl.</u>
2 What's inside the snake bowl? _____
3 What does Diggory use to get Brutus out? _____
4 Who has the Baloney Stone now? _____
5 What's the dog? _____
6 Who does Brutus push into the snake bowl? _____

2 Correct the sentences.

1 At first, Brutus thought that the animal felt like a mouse.
<u>At first, Brutus thought that the animal felt like a spider.</u>

2 The dangerous ancient trap is called a "snake plate."
_____

3 Brutus loves spiders.
_____

4 The snake didn't wake up.
_____

5 Diggory used his scarf to help Brutus out of the snake bowl.
_____

6 Brutus thought the dog was the window.
_____

Do you remember?

1 A lemon sometimes _____looks_____ like a lime.
2 Pizza doesn't smell _____ spaghetti.
3 You need a spoon and a _____ to eat spaghetti.
4 You need an _____ to cook pizza.
5 Underline the stressed words: "Put your hand into this box."
6 Underline the stressed words: "What does it feel like?"

Can do

I can talk about the five senses.

I can plan a party.

I can write about my favorite meal.

How do we make noises?

1 **Read and circle the sound words.**

Sounds I hate to hear

I hate to hear a loud bell (clanging) because it gives me a headache.

I hate to hear an angry lion roaring because it makes me feel scared.

I hate to hear car horns honking outside my house because it wakes me up in the morning.

But I love to hear the first school bell ringing because it means I'll see my friends!

2 **Plan to write a poem. Complete the information about sounds you love and hate.**

Sounds I love to hear)))

I love to hear _____ because it means _____.

I love to hear _____ because it means _____.

I love to hear _____ because it makes me feel _____.

I love to hear _____ because it makes me feel _____.

But I hate to hear _____ because _____.

3 **Use your notes to write a poem.**

4 **Did you ...**

- [ ] plan your poem?
- [ ] use sound words?
- [ ] read your poem again?
- [ ] check grammar, spelling, and punctuation?

Writing tip

Sound words sound like their meanings. You can use them in your poem to help the reader hear the sounds you are writing about.

I hate to hear lions **roaring** because it makes me feel scared.

I love to hear plates **clattering** in the kitchen because it means dinner is almost ready.

Flyers Reading and Writing

1 **Look at the picture and read the story. Write some words to complete the sentences about the story. You can use 1, 2, 3, or 4 words.**

Helen is twelve, and she has a brother named William, who's six. Last Saturday, Helen's dad took them to an art museum downtown. They were very happy. There was a show of modern art by a famous artist, and the museum was full of people. Helen was standing in front of a painting, looking at it when William said, "This looks like a really big pizza with small tomatoes and olives on it."

Helen said, "You don't understand modern art, William. This is a great painting that shows us that life is beautiful, but difficult." Helen's dad laughed and said, "I think William understands modern art better than you, Helen. Look!" Helen's dad pointed, and Helen saw the title of the painting. It was called *Pizza with Tomatoes and Olives*.

Example

Helen's brother _____is six_____ years old.

Questions

1 Helen has _____ named William.

2 Last Saturday, Helen and William _____ art museum with their father.

3 The show was by a famous artist, and there were a lot of _____ in the museum.

4 One painting _____ like a really big pizza.

5 Helen's dad pointed to the title of the _____ .

Review Units 5 and 6

1 Read the story. Choose the words from the box to complete the sentences.

~~competition~~ felt flour like made movie
pizzas plastic sounded touch were

FRIENDLY

Last November, Frankie won an important art (1) _competition_ for her painting *Modern Girl*, which she said looked (2) _____ Jenny. The prize was a meal for two at Luigi's, the town's best Italian restaurant.

Frankie invited Jenny to have lunch with her. Jenny was very happy. She bought a new dress, which was (3) _____ of bright yellow wool. She wore it with a big brown (4) _____ belt and a dark brown jacket. She looked like a "modern girl," and she (5) _____

like a movie star. The two friends felt hungry when they arrived at the restaurant. The waiter put their (6) _____ on the table, and they agreed they smelled like the best pizzas in the world. When they were eating them, they said they tasted like nothing on Earth – they were delicious. After the pizza, Luigi came out of the kitchen and carefully put the second course on the table. It was his most famous dessert, "Banana and Chocolate Surprise." Frankie and Jenny felt very surprised. It looked just like Jenny's clothes!

2 Choose a title for this episode of *Friendly*.

a The cook's famous clothes   b A sweet dress   c Jenny looks like a pear

3 Find the one that is not like the others and write why.

1 silver   metal   gold   (plastic)
Plastic – because it isn't a metal.

2 salt   olives   wool   pepper
_____

3 eyes   feel   taste   smell
_____

4 spoon   bracelet   knife   fork
_____

5 wool   hair   stone   fur
_____

6 wood   paper   cardboard   glass
_____

4 **Complete the sentences. Count and write the letters.**

1 Her smartphone _____sounds_____ like a baby laughing. `6`

2 We have five senses. They are sight, hearing, touch, smell, and _____ . ☐

3 We use a _____ to cut meat. ☐

4 _____ is a material we get from sheep. ☐

5 The opposite of "strong" is _____ . ☐

6 What does that cloud look _____ ? ☐

7 We hear with our _____ . ☐

8 We use a _____ to eat soup. ☐

9 _____ is an expensive white metal. ☐

10 Knives and forks can be made of metal or _____ . ☐

11 _____ is a material we get from trees. ☐

12 What's your bracelet _____ of? Metal. ☐

13 We feel _____ if we don't drink. ☐

14 We serve food on a _____ . ☐

5 **Now complete the crossword. Write the message.**

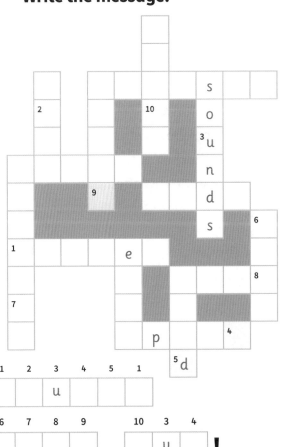

6 **Quiz time!**

1 What's Robert's spider made of?
Robert's spider is made of fur.

2 What's Arsenault's house made of?
_____

3 Where is the *Giant Faucet* sculpture?
_____

4 What smells like Robert's socks?
_____

5 What does Luigi's Italian restaurant make?
_____

6 What's the loudest sound on Earth?
_____

7 **Write questions for your quiz in your notebook.**

7 Natural world

We use *should* to give and ask for help or advice.

Affirmative	Negative (n't = not)	Question
I **should take care of** nature.	You **shouldn't throw** trash on the ground.	**Should** he **help** his mom in the backyard?
She **should clean up** her room.	We **shouldn't forget** that we only have one world.	**Should** they **drive** a big car?

1 Read and match.

1 What should you wear if you go for a long walk?
2 What should you wear outdoors on a sunny day?
3 What should you wear when it's very cold?
4 Who should you ask for help if you get lost in a big city?
5 What should you do when you cross the street?
6 Why should you use sunblock?

☐ You should wear a coat and scarf.
☐ You should stop and look both ways.
[1] You should wear good shoes.
☐ To protect your skin from the sun.
☐ You should ask a police officer.
☐ You should wear a hat.

2 Think and write "should" or "shouldn't."

1 It's a sunny day, and Yu Xi's at the beach. She ____should____ wear a hat.
2 Michael has a headache. He _____ watch TV.
3 Nadia has a terrible toothache. She _____ go to the dentist.
4 Fahad wants to cross the street. He _____ stop and look both ways first.
5 Anika _____ eat chocolate because she has a stomachache.
6 Hiroto has an important test tomorrow, so he _____ study this afternoon.

3 Correct the sentences.

1 We've should take care of nature. We should take care of nature.
2 We should to walk on the paths. _____
3 We should drop our trash on the ground. _____
4 We always should use recycling bins. _____
5 We shouldn't of play with animals in fields. _____
6 We's shouldn't drink water from rivers. _____

▶ Do the online activities on **Practice Extra** as you complete this unit.

1 Match the problems to the correct advice.

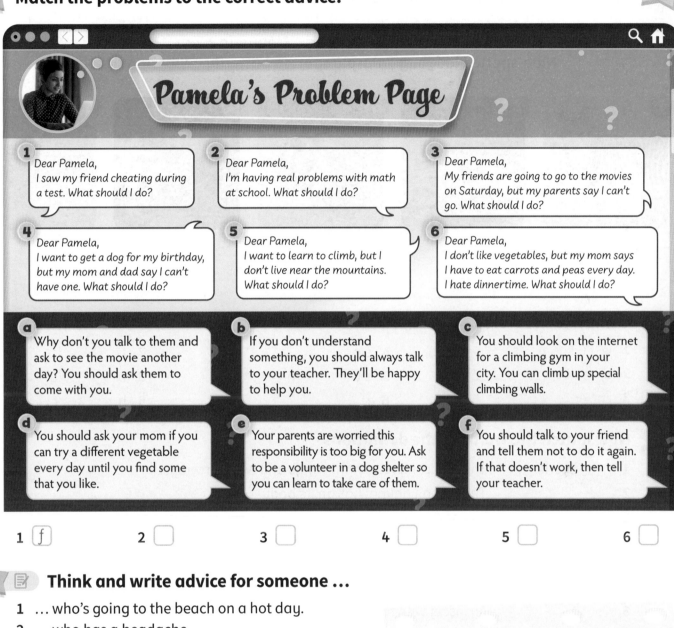

Pamela's Problem Page

1 Dear Pamela,
I saw my friend cheating during a test. What should I do?

2 Dear Pamela,
I'm having real problems with math at school. What should I do?

3 Dear Pamela,
My friends are going to go to the movies on Saturday, but my parents say I can't go. What should I do?

4 Dear Pamela,
I want to get a dog for my birthday, but my mom and dad say I can't have one. What should I do?

5 Dear Pamela,
I want to learn to climb, but I don't live near the mountains. What should I do?

6 Dear Pamela,
I don't like vegetables, but my mom says I have to eat carrots and peas every day. I hate dinnertime. What should I do?

a Why don't you talk to them and ask to see the movie another day? You should ask them to come with you.

b If you don't understand something, you should always talk to your teacher. They'll be happy to help you.

c You should look on the internet for a climbing gym in your city. You can climb up special climbing walls.

d You should ask your mom if you can try a different vegetable every day until you find some that you like.

e Your parents are worried this responsibility is too big for you. Ask to be a volunteer in a dog shelter so you can learn to take care of them.

f You should talk to your friend and tell them not to do it again. If that doesn't work, then tell your teacher.

1 [f] 2 [ ] 3 [ ] 4 [ ] 5 [ ] 6 [ ]

2 Think and write advice for someone …

1 … who's going to the beach on a hot day.
2 … who has a headache.
3 … who wants to learn English.
4 … who wants to try a new hobby.
5 … who wants to learn more about the past.
6 … who is always fighting with their brother.

1 You should take a hat and sunblock.
You shouldn't lie in the sun all day.

3 Answer the questions.

1 Do your friends talk to you when they have a problem? _____
2 Do you help your friends? _____
3 Do you think you should always keep secrets? _____
4 Who do you talk to when you have a problem? _____
5 What are the biggest problems for you and your friends? _____
6 When should you tell your teacher about a problem? _____

Choose the words from the box to label the pictures.

> Lehmann's poison frog ~~Mountain zebra~~
> Nine-spotted ladybug   Purple spotted butterfly   Siberian tiger

Mountain
zebra

Complete the words.

1 w _i_ n _g_ _s_
2 b _ tt _ f _ _
3 i n _ _ c _

4 s p _ _ _
5 s t _ _ p _
6 f _ _ _

7 t _ _ l
8 b _ _ y
9 b _ _ t l _

Now match the words to the definitions.

1 _beetle_   This insect has two hard wings and two soft wings.
2 _____   The hair an animal has on its body.
3 _____   The parts of an insect or animal that it uses to fly.
4 _____   Lions, tigers, elephants, and mice all have one of these. It comes out of
         the back part of their bodies.
5 _____   The part of an animal or insect that has the arms and legs on it.
6 _____   An insect with two beautiful wings, six legs, and two antennae.
7 _____   A small animal with a body, six legs, and two eyes.
8 _____   A small colored circle on a different color.
9 _____   An area between two lines that is a different color.

Write the words in the table.

> across   appear   ~~become~~   explore   extinct   extinction   ~~funny~~
> into   over   recycle   ~~spot~~   spotted   stripe   striped   ~~through~~   wing

Adjectives	Verbs	Prepositions	Nouns
funny	become	through	spot

Match the pictures of endangered animals to the words.

 a
 b
 c d

 e
 f
 g
 h

1 Leatherback turtle [a]
2 Orangutan [ ]
3 White rhino [ ]
4 Iberian lynx [ ]

5 Whale [ ]
6 Giant panda [ ]
7 Bearded vulture [ ]
8 Bat [ ]

2 Find out one fact about each of the endangered animals in Activity 1.

Leatherback turtles live in the Pacific Ocean.

3 **Now make a quiz for your friends.**

Endangered animals quiz

1 Where do leatherback turtles live?

4 Read and order the story.

[ ] "What's your question?" the teacher asked.

[ ] The old man said, "I don't know, either. Here are your two dollars!"

[1] One day, a very smart teacher went to a small town in the country.

[ ] The teacher was happy with the old man's idea because he was very smart.

[ ] The teacher thought for a long time, but he didn't know the answer.

[ ] "What animal has three heads, two wings, and one leg?" the old man asked.

[ ] He was talking to the people there when an old man spoke to him: "I have a question for you. If you can't answer my question, you give me ten dollars. Then you ask me a question. If I can't answer it, I give you two dollars."

[ ] After thinking for 30 minutes, he gave the old man his ten dollars and said, "I'm sorry. I don't know the answer. What is it?"

Sounds and life skills
Taking care of your community
Pronunciation focus

 24 Listen and circle the stressed words.

1 We should (clean up) the beach.
2 People should pick up their trash.
3 People should put plastic trash in the yellow bins.
4 We should ask the government for bags.
5 People shouldn't leave trash on the beach.
6 Where should people throw the trash?

 Circle to complete the rules.

We don't say every word in a sentence with the same force. Strong words are important words, so we say them with more force.

Verbs, adjectives, and nouns **are / are not** strong words.

Prepositions (*in*, *on*, *at*) **are / are not** strong words.

Negative words (*shouldn't*, *don't*, *didn't*) **are / are not** strong words.

 25 Listen and complete.

Lola: Look at this beach! There's so much trash!
Li Wei: We ___should___ do something!
Fahad: _____ _____ clean it up?
Lola: Good idea! We _____ ask more friends to help.
Fahad: _____ message them. We could meet next Saturday morning.
Nadia: My mom works with the government. I _____ ask for some trash bags and gloves.
Li Wei: Great! _____ _____ we also take pictures and send them to the local newspaper?
Lola: Yes! Then people will be more responsible!

 Complete Lola's message.

~~beach~~   clean   clean-up
Great   newspaper   pictures

Hi helpers!
Just want to say a BIG thank you for all your help at the
(1) ___beach___ last weekend.
It looks so (2) _____
now! We took a lot of
(3) _____ to send to
our local (4) _____, *The Evening Report*. Everyone should see how important it is to work together in the community!
Let's start planning our next
(5) _____ in Chestnut
Woods!
(6) _____ job, everyone!
Thanks again,
The Neighborhood Clean-up Team!

7

1 Read and answer.

Diggory Bones

1 What animal does Bones say Brutus is? He says he's a snake.
2 Why should Emily go down the ladder slowly and carefully? _____
3 Where does the ladder take them? _____
4 Describe the butterflies. _____
5 What shouldn't Brutus do? _____
6 What's inside the box? _____

2 Read and order the text.

At the foot of the ladder, there was a big room full of butterflies. ☐

Diggory jumped into the snake bowl to save Emily. 1

Thousands of butterflies flew off the walls to protect their young. ☐

The box was full of striped insects, so Brutus yelled, "Aagh!" ☐

There was a ladder under the door. They climbed slowly and carefully down it. ☐

When Diggory and Emily were looking at the butterflies, Brutus opened a box. ☐

Diggory knew how to get out. He opened a secret door. ☐

The room was the famous butterfly room of Queen Hetepheres. ☐

Do you remember?

1 I have a problem. What ____should____ I do?
2 You _____ throw trash on the floor. Put it in a trash can.
3 The Lost Ladybug Project asks people to take _____ of these endangered beetles.
4 Two endangered animals that have _____ are tigers and zebras.
5 Underline the strong words: "People shouldn't throw trash in the lake."
6 Underline the strong words: "What should they do with their trash?"

Can do

I can describe insects and animals.

I can talk about things we should or shouldn't do.

I can write about how to take care of our world.

How can we help endangered species?

1 **Read and underline facts with *when*.**

PROTECTING HEDGEHOGS

Hedgehogs are nocturnal animals, which means that they sleep during the day and come out at night. They have very short legs, but they can walk very far. <u>When they come out at night for food, they can walk more than 3 kilometers!</u>

They have around 5,000 spikes, and when they're scared, their spikes rise up to protect them. Hedgehogs eat mostly insects and earthworms. One reason why hedgehogs are endangered is that when humans use pesticides to kill insects, there are fewer insects for the hedgehogs to eat.

When hedgehogs come into your yard, you should give them cat or dog food because this is healthy for them. When hedgehogs drink milk, they get very sick, so you should never give it to them.

2 **Plan to write a report. Complete the information about an endangered animal.**

Title	Protecting _____
Why are _____ important?	_____ are so important because _____.
	When _____, _____.
Why are they endangered?	They're endangered because _____.
	When _____, _____.
	That means the number of _____ in the world is going down.
How can we help?	We can help by _____. I think we should _____, but we shouldn't _____.

3 **Use your notes to write a report about the endangered animal.**

4 **Did you ...**
- [ ] plan your report?
- [ ] give facts with ***when***?
- [ ] read your report again?
- [ ] check grammar, spelling, and punctuation?

Writing tip

We use ***when*** to give facts. You can use ***when*** in your report to talk about your animal and what it does.

When hedgehogs come out for food, they can walk more than 3 kilometers.

Flyers Listening

Listen and draw lines. There is one example.

Betty   Harry   Richard   George

Katy   Holly   Sarah

8 World of sports

We use the present perfect to talk and write about experiences and things we did recently.

Affirmative	Negative (n't = not)	Question
I**'ve played** tennis.	You **haven't played** volleyball.	**Has** he **played** basketball?
She**'s been** to Japan twice.	We **haven't been** invited.	**Have** they **been** sick?

1 Are these verbs regular or irregular? Write "R" or "I."

arrive ___R___ lose ___I___ believe _____ make _____ stop _____ play _____

meet _____ catch _____ jump _____ win _____ finish _____ wash _____

2 Make negative sentences.

1 I've sailed from England to Ireland.
   I haven't sailed from England to Ireland.

2 She's won a prize.
   _____

3 They've played basketball.
   _____

4 He's climbed the highest mountain.
   _____

5 You've won the game.
   _____

6 We've made a kite.
   _____

3 Match the pictures to the text.

It's the first time she's played badminton!

This is the first time you've worked in a restaurant, isn't it?

It's the first time he's won a prize. [1]

Is this the first time they've washed the car?

I've never made a cake before.

We've never been ice-skating before.

Do the online activities on **Practice Extra** as you complete this unit.

1 Answer the questions.

1 What's the third letter in "heard"? _a_

2 What's the second letter in "climbed"? _____

3 What's the fifth letter in "stopped"? _____

4 What's the first letter in "hockey"? _____

5 What's the third letter in "skated"? _____

6 What's the first letter in "badminton"? _____

7 What's the sixth letter in "started"? _____

8 What's the sixth letter in "basketball"? _____

What's the word? _____

2 Now make your word puzzle.

1 What's the seventh letter in "basketball"? _____

2 What's the first letter in "appeared"? _____

3 Write the correct form of the verbs in the email.

Hi Freya,

I'm writing to tell you about the things I've ⁽¹⁾ _done_ (do) in the last month or two. We haven't ⁽²⁾ _____ (talk) for two months. I'm sorry, but I've been really busy. I've ⁽³⁾ _____ (study) a lot because I have tests next week, and at last I've ⁽⁴⁾ _____ (finish) the book that you gave me for my birthday. It was really interesting.

Let me tell you what's ⁽⁵⁾ _____ (happen) at the sports club. You know that I was on the tennis team, don't you? Well, I've ⁽⁶⁾ _____ (decide) to change sports. I've ⁽⁷⁾ _____ (stop) playing tennis, and now I've ⁽⁸⁾ _____ (start) bike racing. It's very difficult, but I like it. I've ⁽⁹⁾ _____ (race) twice, and I finished fifth and ninth. Not bad, really. Look at the picture! I'm in it!

Have you ever ⁽¹⁰⁾ _____ (win) a race?

Write soon!
Danny

4 Look at the pictures. Write the questions.

8

What have they done? _____

_____

_____

_____

_____

_____

5 Now answer the questions.

1 They've arrived in London.

2 _____

3 _____

4 _____

5 _____

6 _____

Look and complete the words.

 s k i i n g

 s _ _ w b _ _ _ d i _ _

 _ _ l _ d _ _ _ _

 c _ _ l _ _ _

 t r _ _ k a _ _ f _ _ l _

 _ _ _ _ f

 Write the seasons.

1 This is the hottest season. _____summer_____

2 In this season, all the new flowers start growing. _____

3 This is the season when trees lose their leaves. _____

4 This is the coldest season. This season comes after fall. _____

 Write the sports words in the table.

> basketball   cycling   horseback riding   ice hockey   ice-skating
> Ping-Pong   sailing   skiing   sledding   ~~soccer~~   tennis   track and field

Winter sports	Ball sports	Other sports
	soccer	

 What are the sports? Write the words in the puzzle.

1 | h | o | r | s | e | b | a | c | k | riding

2

3

4 roller-

5

6 | y |

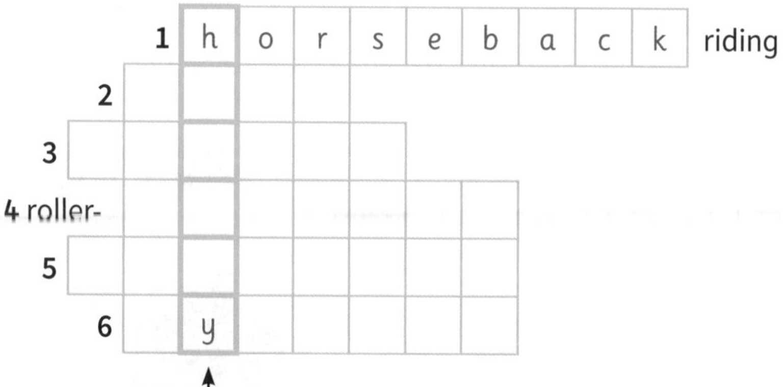

What's the mystery sport? _____

1 Read and write the sports.

> basketball   golf   ~~Ping Pong~~   sailing   snowboarding   waterskiing

1 You play it inside with a small ball, two paddles, and a table.   Ping-Pong

2 This is a team game. Each team has five players. In this sport, you can bounce, throw, and catch the big ball.

_____

3 You do this sport on mountains when there is snow. You have to stand up to do it. _____

4 You do this sport on water. You need a boat. _____

5 You can do this on the ocean or on a lake. You stand up and a boat pulls you.

_____

6 This is not a team game, and you have to play outside. The players hit a very small ball around a course with 18 holes.

2 📝 Now write definitions for six more sports.

1 You usually do this sport outside. You need a bicycle.

3 Read and complete the table.

Three friends live in houses 1, 2, and 3, next to each other on Ice Road, and they have made a snowman. Where does each friend live? What has each child brought to put on the snowman?

Robert lives at number 3. He didn't bring a carrot for the snowman's nose. Sally brought a scarf for the snowman. Richard doesn't live next to Robert. One of the boys brought a hat for the snowman.

Name			Robert
House number			
Thing for the snowman			

4 Choose the words. Then draw your snowman in your notebook.

Last weekend, it was very cold, and it snowed a lot. We went outside to play in the **park / forest / yard**. First we **played / jumped / sledded** in the snow. Then we decided to make a **big / small / tall / fat / funny / thin** snowman.

When we finished making it, we gave it a **carrot / banana / pear** for a nose and some **leaves / rocks / stones** for a mouth. Then we put an old **brown / red / purple** hat on its head and a long **polka-dot / striped** scarf around its neck. The scarf was **blue and green / pink and purple / red and yellow**. Finally we put two **orange / gray / black** gloves on sticks and put them into its body. The gloves were made of **leather / wool / rubber**. Our snowman looked **happy / sad / surprised / angry / amazing**. We called it

_____ .

Sounds and life skills
Working together
Pronunciation focus

 27 Circle the word with a different -ed sound. Listen and check.

1 opened   listened   (helped)   rained
2 stopped   arrived   crossed   jumped
3 looked   picked   cooked   cleaned

4 worked   invited   wanted   waited
5 finished   painted   washed   watched

 28 Listen and circle the correct -ed sound.

1 We've climbed the highest wall in the sports center.   (/d/) /t/
2 I've finished my homework.   /d/ /t/
3 I've opened the door for my mom.   /d/ /t/
4 We've picked up the trash on the beach.   /d/ /t/
5 My brother's cooked pasta for dinner.   /d/ /t/
6 We've listened to music together.   /d/ /t/
7 My sister and I have washed our grandpa's car.   /d/ /t/

 Match and write for each picture.

~~Are you alright?~~   I can clean the kitchen.   Let's work together!
Would you like some help?   You're welcome!

1

Are you alright?

2

If you clean the living room,
.

3

Thank you so much!

4

 29 Read and complete with a verb from Activity 1. Listen and check.

1 Today I've _____ helped _____ my younger brother with his homework.
2 Today we've _____ our house.
3 Today I've _____ some clothes for my grandma.
4 Today we've _____ on a project together.

1 Read and answer.

Diggory Bones

1 Why shouldn't Brutus open his mouth? <u>The butterflies are dangerous.</u>
2 Has Diggory ever used the new door? _____
3 Which sports did the Ancient Egyptians invent? _____
4 Where did Diggory send the email from? _____
5 What does the ancient story of Sirius say? _____
_____

2 Who said it? Read and match.

a They've painted sports on these walls. 3

b It's the first time anyone's used this door.

c I've waited for this moment all my life.

d Now what have you done?

e I haven't touched anything.

f You're the "treasure" now, Brutus!

Do you remember?

1 Have you ever _____been_____ to Egypt?
2 He's _____ the race. Now he can celebrate!
3 They haven't _____ badminton before.
4 _____ is the season that comes after spring.
5 Two words with the /t/ ending (as in "cross__ed__") are _____ and _____ .
6 Two words with the /d/ ending (as in "climb__ed__") are _____ and _____ .

Can do

I can talk about things I have done.

I can talk about different sports.

I can write about different sports.

How do people train for different sports?

1 **Read and complete.**

Another reason   ~~First of all~~   Lastly   Secondly

SKIING

It's never too late to try skiing, especially if you live near snowy mountains, and there are a lot of reasons why it's such an amazing sport.
(1) _____First of all_____ , it's an aerobic activity, which means that it helps keep you healthy. (2) _____ , it's a great way to meet people, and it's the perfect sport to do in a group.
(3) _____ is that it's very good for your mental health to be in the fresh air, looking at beautiful mountains while you exercise.
(4) _____ , it's a lot of fun to be able to move quickly down the mountain.

2 **Plan to write a brochure. Complete the information about an amazing sport.**

AMAZING SPORTS

Try _____!
It's never too late to try _____, and there are a lot of reasons why it's such an amazing sport.
Firstly, _____ .
Secondly, _____ .
Another reason you should try _____ is _____ .
Finally, _____ .

3 **Use your notes to write a brochure about the sport.**

4 **Did you ...**

- ☐ plan your brochure?
- ☐ organize your ideas?
- ☐ read your brochure again?
- ☐ check grammar, spelling, and punctuation?

Writing tip

We use *firstly, first of all, secondly, another reason is, lastly,* and *finally,* to organize ideas. You should use these in your writing because they help the reader understand your ideas more clearly.

First of all, it's an aerobic activity, which means that it helps keep you healthy.

Secondly, it's a good way to meet people.

Physical education: aerobic and anaerobic exercise |  critical thinking

Flyers Reading and Writing

1 **Read the text. Choose the right words and write them on the lines.**

Winter sports

Example	Winter sports are sports _____that_____ people do on snow or
1	ice. _____ sports are very popular in countries where it's
2	really cold _____ winter. One of the most enjoyable winter
3	sports is skiing. There _____ three kinds of
4	_____ at the Olympic Games today. One is downhill skiing,
5	where _____ race down a hill. In another
6	kind, competitors _____ on snowy trails. They can race for
7	up to 50 kilometers. The _____ kind is ski jumping, which is very
8	_____ . Skating, snowboarding, and sledding are just some
9	_____ the other winter sports. At the Winter
10	Olympic Games, there are _____ than ten different sports.

Example	who	when	that				
1	This	That	These	**6**	racing	race	races
2	in	at	on	**7**	third	three	thirty
3	is	are	was	**8**	excited	excites	exciting
4	skied	skiing	skying	**9**	of	at	over
5	people	person	persons	**10**	most	much	more

1 **Read the story. Choose the words from the box to complete the sentences.**

> are   coming   done   ~~ever~~   ride   skis
> sled   snowman   taking   was   were

FRIENDLY

Have you (1) _____ever_____ been skiing? This is what happened to Jim and Sally when they went last winter.

Last January, the five friends went skiing with their class. On the first day, Frankie, Peter, and Jenny decided that it was too dangerous for them, so they chose a sled and found somewhere nice and quiet at the bottom of the mountain to (2) _____ on it. Jim and Sally got their skis and went quickly to the ski lift, which was taking the other skiers to the top of the mountain. It was Sally's first time on a ski lift, but Jim told her it was easy and she felt really excited. They sat on the thin metal seat, held the long piece of metal that was between them, and the lift started. When they (3) _____ going up the mountain, Sally fell off. She fell onto her face and stomach with her skis crossed behind her, and she couldn't move. The other skiers, who were coming up on the lift behind her, couldn't stop and fell off, too. Sally took her (4) _____ off to move out of the way, but she dropped them and they quickly slid down the mountain.

Frankie, Peter, and Jenny, who were sledding happily at the bottom of the mountain, suddenly saw Sally's skis coming, but they couldn't do anything and the skis hit their (5) _____. They all fell off into the snow.

On the second day, the friends decided to do something safer. They made a (6) _____!

2 **Choose a title for this episode of *Friendly*.**

   a Snow feels cold   **b** Snowy disaster!   **c** Summer vacations

3 **Match the questions to the answers.**

  1 What can you catch but not throw?

  2 Waiter! Waiter! What's this fly doing on my ice cream?

  3 Where do horses go when they are sick?

  4 What's worse than finding an insect in your apple?

  5 What goes "tick tock woof tick tock woof"?

  6 Why was 10 afraid of 7?

☐	A watchdog.
☐	Because 7 ate 9.
☐	I think it's skiing, sir.
1	A cold.
☐	To a horspital.
☐	Finding only half an insect in your apple.

4 Complete the sentences. Count and write the letters.

1 Snowboarding isn't easy. It's very ___difficult___ . ⑨

2 Have you _____ won a prize? No, never. ☐

3 When a plant or animal species doesn't exist anymore, it's _____ . ☐

4 He's _____ his homework, so now he can watch TV. ☐

5 They aren't running anymore. They've _____ . ☐

6 What _____ they done? They've washed the car. ☐

7 When we have a picnic, we _____ pick up our trash. ☐

8 The T. rex is an extinct _____ . ☐

9 Animals that fly need two _____ . ☐

10 He's the winner. He's _____ higher than the other jumpers. ☐

11 The Olympic _____ take place every four years. ☐

12 Zebras have black and white _____ on their fur. ☐

13 Animal hair is called _____ . ☐

14 You play _____ on grass, hitting a small ball into holes with a long stick. ☐

5 Now complete the crossword. Write the message.

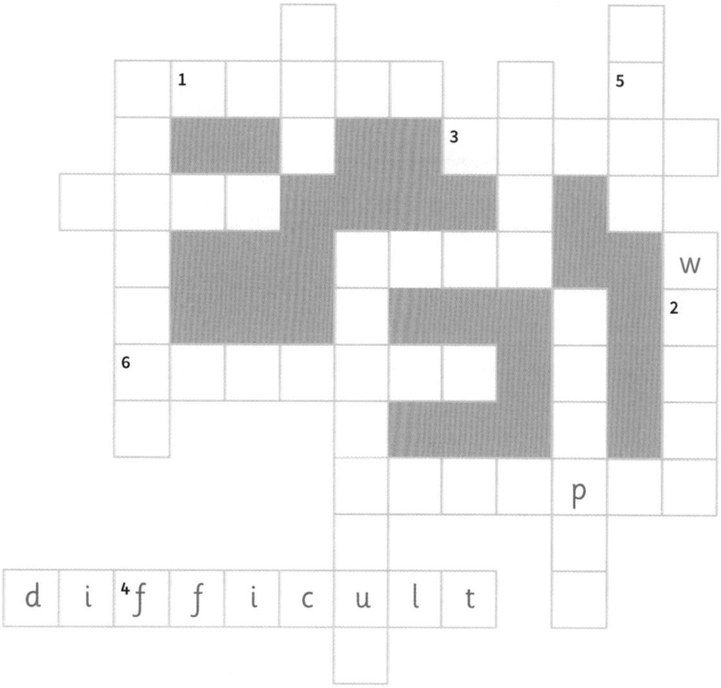

			1						5		

(crossword grid)

1   3   w 2   6   p

d	i	⁴f	f	i	c	u	l	t

1	2	3	1		4	2	5	6	
					f				**!**

6 Quiz time!

1 What should people do with their trash?
They should _____

2 What has two soft and two hard wings?
_____

3 Where do turtles lay their eggs?
_____

4 How many prizes has Robert won?
_____

5 When do people go skiing?
_____

6 What sends oxygen around your body to your muscles?
_____

7 📝 Write questions for your quiz in your notebook.

Respect in the classroom

1 **Read and choose the answer.**

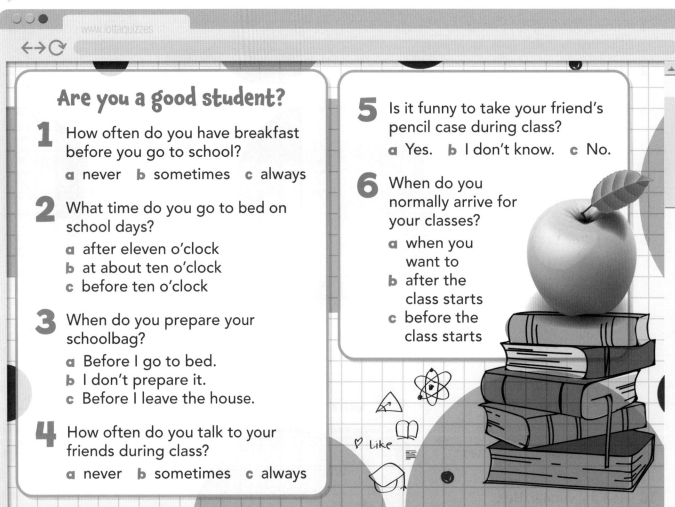

Are you a good student?

1 How often do you have breakfast before you go to school?

a never   b sometimes   c always

2 What time do you go to bed on school days?

a after eleven o'clock
b at about ten o'clock
c before ten o'clock

3 When do you prepare your schoolbag?

a Before I go to bed.
b I don't prepare it.
c Before I leave the house.

4 How often do you talk to your friends during class?

a never   b sometimes   c always

5 Is it funny to take your friend's pencil case during class?

a Yes.   b I don't know.   c No.

6 When do you normally arrive for your classes?

a when you want to
b after the class starts
c before the class starts

♡ Like

2 **Write a class contract.**

1 We have to arrive on time.
2
3
4
5
6 When we do all these things, we can:
  •
  •

1 Read and order the text.

	his car. Firefighters had to cut the car door
	accident. An ambulance took Harry
	much better. He's going to leave the
	had a bad car accident. His car hit a
	the hospital, a team of doctors and
	officers called the hospital and
	Harry's life. Now, two weeks later, Harry is
	truck, and he couldn't get out of
	told the nurses about Harry and his
	which helped stop traffic. At
	to the hospital with a police car behind it,
	nurses worked together to save
1	Last week, Adam's dad, Harry,
	hospital and go home to his family.
	and pull Harry out. Police

2 Write an email to thank the people who saved Harry.

| accident | Best wishes | great job | help |
| now better | operate | save life | two weeks ago |

Imagine that you are Adam. Write a letter to say thank you to the firefighters, police officers, and doctors who saved your dad's life. Use these words to help you.

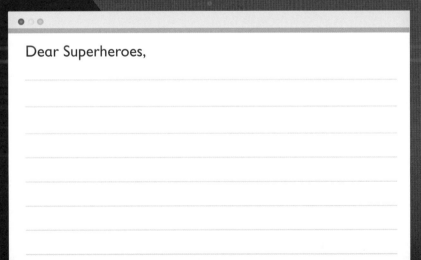

Dear Superheroes,

Tell the truth, but don't hurt

1 Read and answer the questions.

It's always important to tell the truth because it is the right thing to do. But sometimes the truth can hurt, and we don't want to make people feel bad or unhappy. We can still tell the truth without hurting people's feelings. We just need to choose our words very carefully and think before we speak.

1 Why is it important to tell the truth? _____

2 How can telling the truth sometimes make people feel? _____

_____

3 How can we tell the truth without hurting people's feelings? _____

_____

2 Imagine a situation and write about choosing your words carefully.

_____
_____
_____
_____
_____
_____
_____
_____
_____
_____
_____
_____

Units 7&8 Values Value your friendships

1 **Write the sentences and questions.**

1 I / help / can / my / friend? / How How can I help my friend?

2 tell / didn't / I / the / truth. _____

3 talk / should / Who / he / to? _____

4 friend / best / on / cheats / My / tests. _____

5 really / big / made / I've / mistake. / a _____

6 do? / should / I / What _____

2 **Read the letter and answer the questions.**

> Dear Betty and Robert,
>
> I'm worried about my friend, Deniz. He has some new friends at school, and they like doing bad things. Deniz really wants to be part of their group. They told him to go to the shopping mall and steal some things. Deniz doesn't feel that this is wrong. He has started to take little things from a small store near home. He says he's practicing because there are a lot of cameras in the big shopping mall. I told him that these boys aren't really his friends and that the police can catch him, but he doesn't want to listen and laughs at me. He thinks it's a joke. What should I do?
>
> Sincerely yours,
>
> Lucas

1 How can Lucas help Deniz? He should _____

2 Who can Lucas talk to? _____

3 Should Lucas tell Deniz's parents? _____

4 Should Lucas tell a teacher? _____

3 **Write a reply to Lucas.**

_____
_____
_____
_____

Grammar reference

 Write the times.

1 **7:20** Quinn got up at twenty after seven .

2 **7:45** He took a shower at .

3 **7:55** He got dressed at .

4 **8:05** He ate his breakfast at .

5 **8:25** He went to school at .

6 **8:50** He arrived at school at .

 Read and write.

1 They're going to play tennis. (hockey)   No, they aren't. They're going to play hockey.

2 She's going to eat some cheese. (meat)

3 He's going to have lunch at school. (home)

4 We're going to get up early. (late)

5 I'm going to buy a new smartphone. (book)

6 It's going to rain. (snow)

 Read and choose the right words.

1 She rode her bike (**straight down**)/ **left** the street.

2 They drove **past** / **right** the school.

3 He took the fourth street on the **straight ahead** / **right**.

4 The museum was **across** / **corner** the street.

5 I turned **straight ahead** / **left** at the post office.

6 The bus stopped at the **corner** / **across**.

4 Read and order the words.

1   his   George wasn't   homework.   doing
George wasn't doing his homework.

2   in the   Sarah skiing   mountains?   Was

3 I   bath.   taking a   wasn't

_____

4 to an   sailing   island.   David was

_____

5 Emma and Harry   the park.   through   were running

_____

6 the bus stop?   Were   waiting at   you

_____

5 Answer the questions.

1 What are these bowls made of? (silver)   They're made of silver.

2 What's this comic book made of? (paper)   _____

3 What are his shoes made of? (leather)   _____

4 What's her scarf made of? (wool)   _____

5 What are windows made of? (glass)   _____

6 What's that watch made of? (gold)   _____

6 Complete the sentences.

cheese   feel   It   like   ~~tired~~

1 She looked _____tired_____ .

2 They tasted _____ mangoes.

3 It smelled like _____ .

4 We didn't _____ sad.

5 _____ doesn't sound very nice.

7 Read and write "Yes, you should." or "No, you shouldn't."

1 Should you leave your trash on the ground?   No, you shouldn't.

2 Should you play your music very loudly?   _____

3 Should you use sunblock when you go to the beach?   _____

4 Should you play with wild animals?   _____

5 Should you wear good shoes when you hike in the mountains?   _____

6 Should you drink water from a river?   _____

8 Write the questions and answers.

1 she / ever / climb / mountain? (✓)   Has she ever climbed a mountain? Yes, she has.

2 they / ever / enter / competition? (✗)   _____

3 he / ever / play / Ping-Pong? (✗)   _____

4 they / ever / make / snowman? (✓)   _____

5 you / ever / see / the Olympics? (✗)   _____

Irregular verbs

Infinitive	Past tense	Past participle
be	was / were	been
be called	was / were called	been called
be going to	was / were going to	been going to
begin	began	begun
break	broke	broken
bring	brought	brought
buy	bought	bought
can	could	–
catch	caught	caught
choose	chose	chosen
come	came	come
cut	cut	cut
do	did	done
draw	drew	drawn
drink	drank	drunk
drive	drove	driven
eat	ate	eaten
fall	fell	fallen
feel	felt	felt
find	found	found
find out	found out	found out
fly	flew	flown
forget	forgot	forgotten
get	got	gotten
get (un)dressed	got (un)dressed	gotten (un)dressed
get (up / on / off)	got (up / on / off)	gotten (up / on / off)
get to	got to	gotten to
give	gave	given
go	went	gone / been
go out	went out	gone / been out
go shopping	went shopping	gone / been shopping
grow	grew	grown
have	had	had
have to	had to	had to
hear	heard	heard
hide	hid	hidden
hit	hit	hit
hold	held	held
hurt	hurt	hurt
keep	kept	kept

Infinitive	Past tense	Past participle
know	knew	known
leave	left	left
let	let	let
lie down	lay down	lain down
lose	lost	lost
make	made	made
make sure	made sure	made sure
mean	meant	meant
meet	met	met
must	had to	had to
put	put	put
put on	put on	put on
read	read	read
ride	rode	ridden
run	ran	run
say	said	said
see	saw	seen
sell	sold	sold
send	sent	sent
should	–	–
sing	sang	sung
sit	sat	sat
sleep	slept	slept
speak	spoke	spoken
spend	spent	spent
stand	stood	stood
steal	stole	stolen
swim	swam	swum
swing	swung	swung
take	took	taken
take a picture	took a picture	taken a picture
take off	took off	taken off
teach	taught	taught
tell	told	told
think	thought	thought
throw	threw	thrown
understand	understood	understood
wake up	woke up	woken up
wear	wore	worn
win	won	won
write	wrote	written